PALM & TREO HACKS™

Other resources from O'Reilly

Related titles

Treo Fan Book

Wireless Hacks™

Google Hacks™

Linux Unwired

Nokia Smartphone
Hacks™

BlackBerry Hacks™

PC Hacks™

Retro Gaming Hacks™

Astronomy Hacks™

Hacks Series Home

hacks.oreilly.com is a community site for developers and power users of all stripes. Readers learn from each other as they share their favorite tips and tools for Mac OS X, Linux, Google, Windows XP, and more.

oreilly.com

oreilly.com is more than a complete catalog of O'Reilly books. You'll also find links to news, events, articles, weblogs, sample chapters, and code examples.

oreillynet.com is the essential portal for developers interested in open and emerging technologies, including new platforms, programming languages, and operating systems.

Conferences

O'Reilly brings diverse innovators together to nurture the ideas that spark revolutionary industries. We specialize in documenting the latest tools and systems, translating the innovator's knowledge into useful skills for those in the trenches. Visit *conferences.oreilly.com* for our upcoming events.

Safari Bookshelf (*safari.oreilly.com*) is the premier online reference library for programmers and IT professionals. Search across thousands of electronic books simultaneously and zero in on the information you need in seconds. Read the books on your Bookshelf from cover to cover or simply flip to the page you need. You can even cut and paste code and download chapters for offline viewing. Try it today for free.

PALM & TREO HACKS™

Scott MacHaffie

O'REILLY®

Beijing · Cambridge · Farnham · Köln · Paris · Sebastopol · Taipei · Tokyo

Palm and Treo Hacks™
by Scott MacHaffie

Copyright © 2006 O'Reilly Media, Inc. All rights reserved.
Printed in the United States of America.

Published by O'Reilly Media, Inc., 1005 Gravenstein Highway North,
Sebastopol, CA 95472.

O'Reilly books may be purchased for educational, business, or sales promotional use. Online editions are also available for most titles (*safari.oreilly.com*). For more information, contact our corporate/institutional sales department: (800) 998-9938 or *corporate@oreilly.com*.

Editor:	Brian Jepson	**Production Editor:**	Adam Witwer
Series Editor:	Rael Dornfest	**Cover Designer:**	Marcia Friedman
Executive Editor:	Dale Dougherty	**Interior Designer:**	David Futato

Printing History:

October 2005:	First Edition.

 This book uses RepKover,™ a durable and flexible lay-flat binding.

ISBN: 0-596-10054-X
[C]

Contents

Credits

About the Author

Scott MacHaffie (*http://www.nonvi.com/sm*) is a programmer. He learned to program in 1980 and has been getting paid for it since 1987. He has a B.S. and an M.S. in Computer Science, from the University of Washington and Portland State University, respectively. He has studied Human-Computer Interactions and User Interface design for many years. He specializes in GUIs for scientific, engineering, and math applications and is currently working on Maestro, a GUI for chemistry applications, at Schrödinger, Inc. (*http://www.schrodinger.com*). Before that, he worked on geometry software at Saltire Software (*http://www.saltire.com*).

Scott writes games for Palm OS devices as a hobby. He and his wife are learning to speak Irish Gaelic. Scott also teaches aikido when he can get a break from his twin boys, and he is knowledgeable about early Celtic, Irish, and Scottish history.

Contributors

The following people contributed their hacks, writing, and inspiration to this book:

- Jen Edwards, affectionately known as the "PocketGoddess," is the founder and Editor-in-Chief of PocketGoddess.com (*http://www. pocketgoddess.com*), a web site devoted to handheld news and reviews of all kinds. Launched in 2001, the site covers Palm OS, Windows Mobile, smartphones, Apple iPod, and mobile gaming devices such as the Nintendo DS and Sony PSP. As a PalmSource Champion she has authored four Expert Guides to Palm OS software (Life/Time Management, Project Management, Religion: Christianity, and Education: Students) that can be found at *http://www.palmsource.com/applications*. She is also a member of the Palm OS User Council, where she acts as a "voice of the user" to Palm OS platform licensees. Jen is a Staff Writer for Brighthand (*http://www.brighthand.com*) and a freelance writer for a variety of print publications, including *Laptop*, *Computer Power User*, and *CE Lifestyles* magazines.

- Jeff Ishaq (*http://www.ishaq.biz*) is a software engineer and writer living in Santa Cruz, California. He is the author of *Treo Fan Book* for O'Reilly, and has been developing Palm software since 1996. In his spare time, he enjoys eating spicy food, trail running, playing guitar, and alpine snowboarding. He hopes someday to organize his office.

- Brian Jepson is an O'Reilly editor, programmer, and coauthor of *Mac OS X Tiger for Unix Geeks* and *Linux Unwired*. He's also a volunteer systems administrator and all-around geek for AS220 (*http://www.as220.org*), a nonprofit arts center in Providence, Rhode Island. AS220 gives Rhode Island artists uncensored and unjuried forums for their work. These forums include galleries, performance space, and publications. Brian sees to it that technology, especially free software, supports that mission.

Acknowledgments

I would like to thank everyone who helped make *Palm and Treo Hacks* come together. I couldn't have done it without lots of help.

My wife gets first credit for agreeing to let me try writing my first book while we were expecting twin boys. Thank you very much, dear—I love you.

The twins get credit for the hacks that were written at 3 A.M. (a time all good hackers know well). Andrew and Owen loved getting me up early in the morning to feed them a bottle with one hand while writing hacks with the other.

Many thanks go to Brian Jepson, my editor. He provided invaluable text and screenshots for a number of hacks, as well as correcting many of my errors before they made it into print.

I would also like to thank Jeff for doing a great job on the technical review, as well as contributing several cool Treo hacks. Thanks to Jen for providing two nice hacks on interesting ways to use a PDA.

My family has been very supportive and deserves lots of credit. Not only did they provide moral support, but they also took care of the twins regularly so that Nancy and I could have some time to ourselves.

My thanks again to everyone. I hope you enjoy the book!

Preface

Palm devices have evolved over the almost ten years since the first Palm Pilot. The original Palm Pilot had a black-and-white screen with a resolution of 160×160. The only sounds were beeps from a tiny speaker. It had 128KB of RAM and only the basic applications were available (Date Book, Address Book, To Do List, MemoPad, and Calculator). The original Palm Pilots were powered by a pair of AAA batteries and used to last from a week to a month on a single set of batteries, depending on how much you used them (current devices use rechargeable batteries).

Today we have PDAs and smartphones. Color screens of 320×320 or 320×480 are the norm. Palm devices can connect to the world via Bluetooth, Wi-Fi, and cellular data connections. You can listen to music, watch videos, and play games on your Palm device now. Palm devices routinely sport 32MB, and you can get memory cards to boost that to 1GB or more. The LifeDrive comes with a 4GB hard disk. And those basic applications are still there, anchoring Palm devices. The applications have been mostly unchanged. A few tweaks and new features have been added over the past decade, but nothing like the changes in desktop applications over the same period.

Despite all the changes, though, some people insist on seeing Palm devices as merely limited organizers. They point at the built-in applications and say, "I can do all of that with a piece of paper." When that piece of paper can connect to the Internet, then we'll talk. This book will show you how to get more out of your Palm device, whether it is a PDA or a smartphone.

Inside you will find hacks that explore the boundaries of the basic applications. You will also find interesting and novel uses for your Palm device. Not every hack may be useful for you, but they should all be interesting and maybe even entertaining.

So come and explore the world of Palm devices and see what you can learn.

Why Palm and Treo Hacks?

The term *hacking* has a bad reputation in the press. They use it to refer to someone who breaks into systems or wreaks havoc with computers as their weapon. Among people who write code, though, the term *hack* refers to a "quick-and-dirty" solution to a problem, or a clever way to get something done. And the term *hacker* is taken very much as a compliment, referring to someone as being *creative*, having the technical chops to get things done. The Hacks series is an attempt to reclaim the word, document the good ways people are hacking, and pass the hacker ethic of creative participation on to the uninitiated. Seeing how others approach systems and problems is often the quickest way to learn about a new technology.

How to Use This Book

You can read this book from cover to cover if you like, but each hack stands on its own, so feel free to browse and jump to the sections that interest you most. If there's a prerequisite you need to know about, a cross-reference will guide you to the right hack.

How This Book Is Organized

The book is divided into several chapters, organized by subject:

Chapter 1, *Managing Information*
> This chapter explores the dusty corners of the basic applications (Date Book, Address Book, To Do List, and MemoPad). Palm devices are all about information—storing information at a moment's notice and retrieving it later when you need it. These hacks will make you more efficient and help you get the most out of the basic applications.

Chapter 2, *Palm Applications*
> Are you interested in astronomy? Do you manage complicated projects? The applications chapter focuses on using your Palm device to support specialized uses. Each hack covers a single area and shows you how to use your Palm device to support that.

Chapter 3, *Play Games*
> You could write a whole book on gaming hacks (like *Gaming Hacks* by Simon Carless, O'Reilly, 2005). This chapter covers a range of gaming topics from using Palm devices to support traditional pen-and-paper role-playing to multiplayer games to classic games. After all, Palm devices aren't just for work.

Chapter 4, *Multimedia*

A Palm device is really a general-purpose computer. Most people think "PDA" or "smartphone" and limit their expectations. But a Palm device can provide entertainment as well as being a tool for managing information. With a Palm device you can read electronic books, listen to music, or even watch videos. A Palm device may not be as good as a dedicated device for these functions, but it has the advantage of versatility. If you would like to listen to a few songs while still having other functions available, then a Palm device is a better choice than a specialized device like an iPod.

Chapter 5, *Treo*

These hacks revolve around Treo-specific features. The hacks make use of the phone and Internet capabilities of Treos. You can learn how to do web and phone conferencing, or find out how to configure a Treo to match the way you intend to use it.

Chapter 6, *Communications*

How do you connect your Palm device to the Internet? The answer is, it depends. That's why there are hacks devoted to this and related topics. The types of communications available from a Palm device continue to expand. Palm devices now support infrared, Bluetooth, Wi-Fi, and cellular data connections. Your Palm device can talk to the Internet or your stereo, and the hacks in this chapter show you how.

Chapter 7, *System*

System-level hacks get you closer to the underlying Graphical User Interface (GUI) and operating system. You can learn how to tweak the launcher, replace the built-in calculator, or even learn how to write your own programs.

Chapter 8, *Hardware*

Finally, you can get your hands dirty. Do you have problems with the connectors on your Palm device wearing out? Are you looking for cool add-ons or accessories for your Palm device? These are the sorts of things you will find in this chapter.

Conventions

The following is a list of the typographical conventions used in this book:

Italics

Used to indicate URLs, filenames, filename extensions, on-screen options, and directory/folder names. For example, a path in the filesystem will appear as */Developer/Applications*.

Constant width

> Used to show code examples, the contents of files, console output, as well as the names of variables, commands, and other code excerpts.

Constant width bold

> Used to highlight portions of code, typically new additions to old code.

Constant width italic

> Used in code examples and tables to show sample text to be replaced with your own values.

Gray text

> Used to indicate a cross reference within the text.

You should pay special attention to notes set apart from the text with the following icons:

> This is a tip, suggestion, or general note. It contains useful supplementary information about the topic at hand.

> This is a warning or note of caution, often indicating that your money or your privacy might be at risk.

The thermometer icons, found next to each hack, indicate the relative complexity of the hack.

 beginner   moderate   expert

Using Code Examples

This book is here to help you get your job done. In general, you may use the code in this book in your programs and documentation. You do not need to contact us for permission unless you're reproducing a significant portion of the code. For example, writing a program that uses several chunks of code from this book does not require permission. Selling or distributing a CD-ROM of examples from O'Reilly books *does* require permission. Answering a question by citing this book and quoting example code does not require permission. Incorporating a significant amount of example code from this book into your product's documentation *does* require permission.

We appreciate, but do not require, attribution. An attribution usually includes the title, author, publisher, and ISBN. For example: "*Palm and Treo Hacks* by Scott MacHaffie. Copyright 2006 O'Reilly Media, Inc., 0-596-10054-X."

If you feel your use of code examples falls outside fair use or the permission given above, feel free to contact us at *permissions@oreilly.com*.

Safari Enabled®

 When you see a Safari® Enabled icon on the cover of your favorite technology book, that means the book is available online through the O'Reilly Network Safari Bookshelf.

Safari offers a solution that's better than e-books. It's a virtual library that lets you easily search thousands of top tech books, cut and paste code samples, download chapters, and find quick answers when you need the most accurate, current information. Try it for free at *http://safari.oreilly.com*.

How to Contact Us

We have tested and verified the information in this book to the best of our ability, but you may find that features have changed (or even that we have made mistakes!). As a reader of this book, you can help us to improve future editions by sending us your feedback. Please let us know about any errors, inaccuracies, bugs, misleading or confusing statements, and typos that you find anywhere in this book.

Please also let us know what we can do to make this book more useful to you. We take your comments seriously and will try to incorporate reasonable suggestions into future editions. You can write to us at:

O'Reilly Media, Inc.
1005 Gravenstein Highway North
Sebastopol, CA 95472
(800) 998-9938 (in the U.S. or Canada)
(707) 829-0515 (international/local)
(707) 829-0104 (fax)

To ask technical questions or to comment on the book, send email to:

bookquestions@oreilly.com

The web site for *Palm and Treo Hacks* lists examples, errata, and plans for future editions. You can find this page at:

http://www.oreilly.com/catalog/palmtreohks

For more information about this book and others, see the O'Reilly web site:

http://www.oreilly.com

Got a Hack?

To explore Hacks books online or to contribute a hack for future titles, visit:

http://hacks.oreilly.com

Managing Information
Hacks 1–10

The Palm's standard Applications (the built-in applications such as the Date Book, Address Book, MemoPad, and the To Do List) together with the Palm desktop software seem simple, but there are some clever tricks to get the most out of them. The hacks in this section explore the corners of these well-known applications. You may find some new tricks you didn't know about before.

Palm devices, and the standard applications in particular, are models of simplicity. This simplicity came from the careful design of the original team and has been refined over the years. The standard applications work smoothly. For those of us who like to poke around inside the box, however, there are still a few things left to play with. Hopefully you will be surprised by some of these tricks. Some people may know them all, but most people should learn a few new things.

Come and explore what lies inside the standard applications.

HACK #1 Maximize the Date Book

Time—we all look for more time in our busy schedules. Tweaking the built-in Date Book application may not actually create more time, but it can help you manage your time better.

As with the other built-in applications, there are some simple things you can do to get the most out of the Date Book application. Each section in this hack covers a separate tip.

Use the Today View

The Today view shows you any events for the current day, plus any To Do items that are due today, overdue, or unscheduled (see Figure 1-1). You can select the category for the displayed To Do items in the Today view separately from the current category in the To Do List. Otherwise the To Do items follow the preferences that you choose from the Show button in the To Do application (such as whether to show the due date in the view). You can also check off To Do items from the Today view as they are completed.

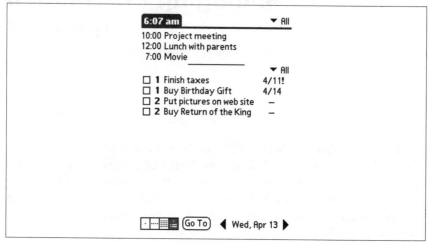

Figure 1-1. Today view in the Date Book

Create Repeating Events

You can set repeating events for birthdays, anniversaries, or regular meetings. You can even set an event to repeat on the fourth Thursday of every other month if you want. To set a repeat, select an event in the daily view and press the Details button. Tap in the field that appears to the right of Repeat. This brings up the Change Repeat dialog box. To get something to repeat the fourth Thursday of every other month (or something similar) select Month and change *Repeat by* to Day. To switch from every month to every other month, change the Every Month(s) field to **2** instead of **1**. The text field at the bottom of the dialog box should change to say The 4th Thursday of every other month, as you can see in Figure 1-2.

So what happens when you modify a repeating event's time or repeat interval? In these cases, you are given a choice to apply the change to the current event only, all, or the current event plus future events. If you choose to apply the changes to the current event and future events, you actually split the event into two events. The original event lasts from the original start date through the date of the event before the one you're editing. Then the current event and future events become a separate repeating event, unconnected to the original event. Any changes you make to the original event will now no longer affect the split event, even if you move the split event back to the same time and repeat interval as the original event.

Figure 1-2. Change Repeat dialog box from the Date Book application

Track To Dos with Floating Events

A *floating event* is a cross between a repeating event and a To Do item. You schedule it like a normal untimed event. A floating event has a circle next to it which acts as the checkbox in the To Do List. You can check the box to mark the floating event as completed. If you pass the date of an uncompleted floating event, then the floating event will continue to show up in your Daily View until you complete it.

Floating events are available standard in the Date Book on some Palm devices. For other devices, you will need to get a replacement application that supports floating events, such as DateBk5 (*http://www.pimlicosoftware.com*). You can see a floating event in DateBk5 in Figure 1-3.

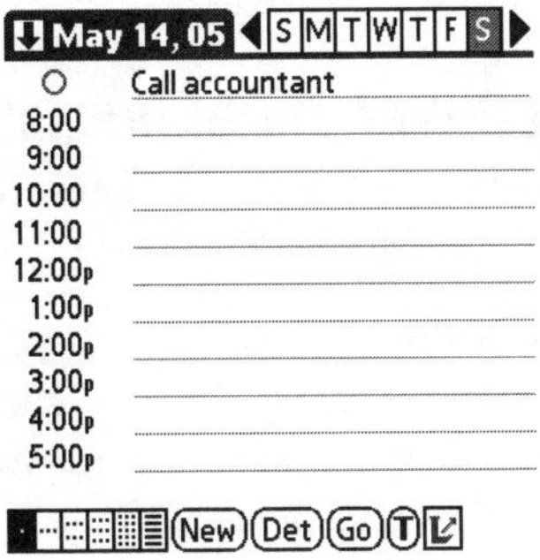

Figure 1-3. Floating event in DateBk5

Just Start Writing

In the Daily view, you can write text to start a new event. If you write a number, the event will start at the corresponding hour. If you write a letter, then a new event will be created as a *No time* event. A No time event is one which comes at the top of the Daily view. It does not reserve any particular time for the event, unlike an all-day event, which takes your normal day's hours (e.g., 8:00 A.M. to 6:00 P.M.).

Purge Events

You can easily remove old events from the Date Book. Go to the Daily view (the one that just displays times, not To Do items). Select Purge from the Record menu. This will bring up a dialog box prompting you to delete items older than one, two, or three weeks, or one month. You can also choose to archive the deleted records on your PC. If you archive the deleted records, then you can view them later in the desktop [Hack #6].

Alarms

You can set alarms on Date Book items by selecting the item and choosing the Details menu item. In the Details dialog box is a checkbox for Alarm. Checking this lets you select how far in advance of the appointment you want to have the alarm go off. The default is five minutes.

In the Prefs application, you can select how you want to be notified. All devices have an option to set the volume of the alarm. Some devices also have other choices for notifying you of an alarm, such as flashing the LED or vibrating.

In Palm OS 6.x, all alarms and alerts (e.g., email and SMS notification) are integrated into the status bar at the bottom of the screen. You can tap on the flashing alert icon to get a display with all of your alarms and alerts.

Get the Most Out of the To Do List

#2

Everyone already knows what you can do with the To Do List. This hack covers things that go a step beyond that.

This hack covers a series of tips and techniques for the built-in To Do List. Some more involved hacks for the To Do List, such as using it for project management [Hack #11] or managing school work [Hack #9], are covered elsewhere in the book and won't be repeated here.

Use Priorities for Grouping

You can use priorities for grouping items within a category (see Figure 1-4). For example, if you have a category like Shopping List, then you might put items from the grocery store as priority 1, hardware store as priority 2, and electronics store as priority 3. Then, each store's items appear together in the list. When you have checked off all the items at the grocery store (priority 1), then you are done with that store. Thus, you will have more time to spend at the hardware store and the electronics store.

```
┌──────────────────────────────────────────────────────┐
│              ┌─────────┐     ▼ Shopping List          │
│              │ To Do   │                              │
│              └─────────┘                              │
│              ☐ 1 Milk                                 │
│              ☐ 1 Eggs                                 │
│              ☐ 1 Bananas                              │
│              ☐ 1 Bread                                │
│              ☐ 2 Hammer                               │
│              ☐ 2 Leaf bags                            │
│              ☐ 2 Primer                               │
│              ☐ 2 Paint brushes                        │
│              ☐ 3 Solder                               │
│              ☐ 3 Case fan                             │
│              ☐ 3 Blank CDs                            │
│              ☐ 3 New monitor                          │
│                                                        │
│                                                        │
│              (New) (Details...) (Show...)             │
└──────────────────────────────────────────────────────┘
```

Figure 1-4. Using priorities for grouping in the To Do List

Priorities in Action

Here is a simple example of priorities. Let's assume that you are going to track CDs to buy, videos to rent, and movies to watch. For this example, the items will be combined into an Entertainment category. I use priorities to distinguish different types of media within the category. Movies will be priority 1, videos 2, and CDs 3. Also, I record movie release dates as the due dates for the items. That way, I will be reminded when new movies are out that I want to watch. You can see how this works in Figure 1-5. You can add titles by giving them a very early date (I used January 1) so that they stay at the top of each section.

So, you can see lots of new ways to use your To Do application besides simply writing down assignments. With some practice, you will find other ways you can use the To Do List.

Use Security as Another Filter

Even if you don't need to use the security feature to protect your data, you still have an opportunity to keep your information private. You can mark some items as Private and then hide or show them all as a group by changing the Security or Privacy settings (depending on which version of Palm OS you are running). One example uses this for speculative items, such as

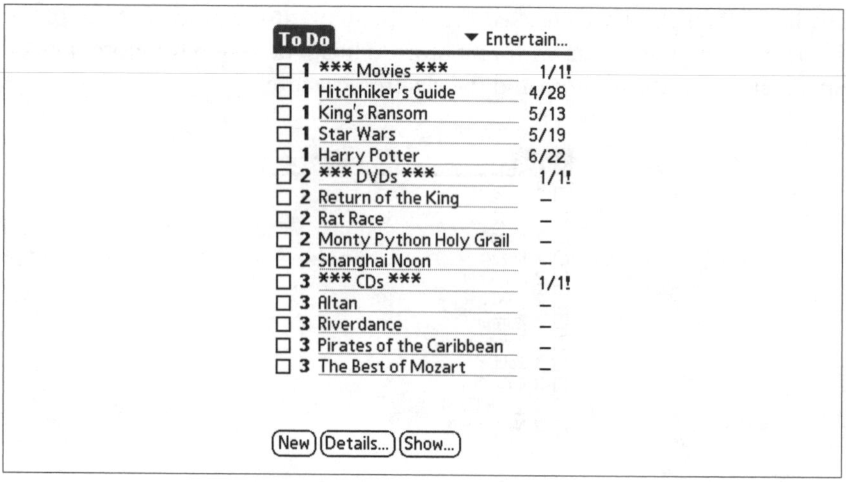

Figure 1-5. Using To Do List to track entertainment

projects at work, gift ideas you are toying with, or some alternate means of accomplishing some of your other tasks. If you mark these items as private, then you can use the Security (Privacy) dialog box to display them by selecting Show Records or hide them by selecting Hide Records, as you can see in Figure 1-6.

Another use for this trick is to mark detailed tasks as private and leave higher-level tasks as public. Then you can use the privacy settings to switch between a detailed view and a higher-level view.

Figure 1-6. Privacy settings in the To Do List

Create a New Item Fast

From the List view, you can start a new item by simply writing in the Graffiti area. This will start a new item in the current category. This trick only saves you one button press, but it is the fastest way to create a new item.

Comparison with the Date Book

Assigning due dates to items is similar to going to the Date Book [Hack #1] application and scheduling an item there. The main advantage of a To Do item over a Date Book item is that the To Do item doesn't disappear when the due date passes unless you explicitly mark it off. In contrast, calendar items only show up on the exact day they are scheduled.

One of the disadvantages of To Do items is that they are not well integrated with the Date Book. The only place To Do items show up in the Date Book is in the Today view. They show up there if they are due today or are over-due (both of these are good) or if they aren't scheduled for a particular date (which means you can end up with a lot of items displayed). However, some Palm devices support floating events [Hack #1] in the Date Book, which keep nagging you until they are done.

Customize the Today View

There are a couple of good alternatives to the Today view for showing your current appointments and To Do items. The standard Date Book provides a Today view which you can tweak a bit [Hack #1]. It has the drawbacks dis-cussed earlier, though: unscheduled items always show up and you can't turn them off.

Two replacement Today views fix this problem and give you the nice addi-tional option of always appearing when you turn on the power to your Palm device. One of these replacements is a HackMaster extension [Hack #47] called TealGlance. TealGlance is purely a Today view—it doesn't have any other functionality.

Another alternative is to replace the standard launcher [Hack #45]. Facer-Launcher provides a Today view that gives you quite a bit of control over what is displayed. It can also integrate data from certain applications into the Today view.

Purging Completed Items

You can easily remove completed items from the To Do List. Select Purge from the Record menu. This will bring up a dialog box asking you to con-firm that you want to delete all completed To Do items. You can also choose whether or not to archive the deleted items. If you archive them, then you can view them later in the desktop [Hack #6].

Extend the Address Book

Just names and phone numbers, right? What could there possibly be to hack in the Address Book? Several small hacks allow you to do more with the Address Book.

As with the To Do List [Hack #2], there are a few simple tricks and techniques you can use to get the most out of the Address Book. These techniques will help you do things that you didn't realize you could do.

Find Jobs and Chase Prospects

You can use the Address Book to ease your job search or make it easier to stay on top of other kinds of prospects. Create a new category called Companies, Prospective Companies, or some such category. Then, add info on companies as you see ads posted by them or as you send them resumes or otherwise contact them. In the Notes section, keep track of job postings (title and date) and any communications you have with the company (sending resumes, interviews, etc.). Note the dates that things happen as well. If you meet with or contact relevant people in the company, add them as separate entries in the Address Book. Keep note of meetings and contacts with them as well. A good use for the Preferences option is to list contacts by company name, last name. Grouping everyone by company can make it easier to keep track of who you have been talking to, which makes it easier to follow up with those contacts.

Find Your Doctors Fast

Write your doctors' names entirely in the last name field to get them to show up correctly. After all, you want to see Dr. Smith show up in the list as Dr. Smith, not Smith, Dr. or just Smith. You can use the title field to indicate what kinds of doctors they are (dentist, family practice, or PhD).

Alternate Business Cards

After you have set up your primary business card, you may want to set up additional business cards. These could be a home address or a side business. Set up a new category titled appropriately. For example, I might create a category called Scott's Card or Scott MacHaffie. Create a single business card for yourself in that category—use one category per card. Then, whenever you want to beam an alternate business card to someone, switch to the appropriate category and select Beam Category from the Record menu. That will send over your alternate business card. You can see examples of doctors, companies, and business cards in Figure 1-7.

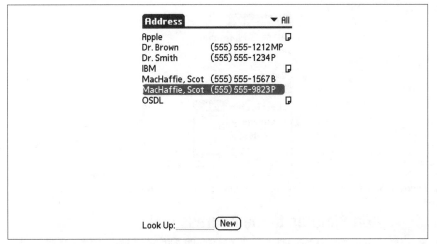

Figure 1-7. Address Book showing companies, doctors, and two business cards

Use Titles as Short Descriptions

You can use the title field as a short description or reminder of who someone is, if you don't need to keep track of an actual title. If you have a restaurant in your address book, you could put a short review in the title—"great ribs" or "order #3." For a person, you might put something like, "Met at Siggraph '05."

Select Which Number to Show

For each item in the Address Book, you can select which phone number is displayed in the List View. You can pick any of the number fields. The number you choose to display is also the number that will be returned if you do a Phone Lookup from one of the other applications. To set the displayed number, select the item from the list view and hit Edit, then select Details. From Details, you can select which number to display under Show in List, as you can see in Figure 1-8.

These numbers don't have to be phone numbers at all. They can be email addresses, web sites, ICQ numbers, or anything else you can think of.

Figure 1-8. Setting the displayed phone number in the Address Book

 HACK
#4

Add Pictures to the Address List

If your Palm device supports it, you can be sure you'll never have trouble putting a name to a face again.

With a couple of easy steps, you can add pictures to the entries in your address list, as you can see in Figure 1-9. You need to have a memory card installed on your Palm device and your Palm needs to support this feature. To check, go to the Address List and tap one of the addresses. Tap Edit. If the Edit page says No Image, then your PDA supports images.

Figure 1-9. Address view, showing a picture

You have a couple of choices. If you are running a PC you can use the Image Converter application to copy files over. You can also just copy the files over directly.

Image Converter

If you want to use Image Converter, then either run it and select images from there, or from the Windows desktop, right-click on images and hit Send To → Image Converter from the pop-up menu.

With Image Converter running, attach your Palm device to the cable or cradle and launch the Data Import application. When Data Import is running, press the Connect button.

 Do not hit Disconnect in the Data Import application while data is being transferred. Doing so could cause you to lose data off of your memory card.

You can select images from Image Converter. When you have all of the images selected that you want to transfer and your Palm device is connected via Data Import, then press the Output button. This will bring up a dialog box that prompts you to save the images to a drive. When you run the Data Import button and hit Connect, Windows treats the memory card as a new drive.

From the save dialog box, you can select the Settings button to resize the images or to fit them to a specific size, as you can see in Figure 1-10. The images that are transferred over are not specific to the Address Book—you can use them for other purposes as well. If you want to size the images specifically for the Address Book, then you are looking at a square size of 88×88 pixels on most devices, although Treos use images of 96×96 pixels. You can also resize images down if they don't look good when squared to other sizes (e.g., 88×66).

Figure 1-10. Settings dialog box in Image Converter

Direct Copying

You can also directly copy files from your desktop machine to the correct location on the memory card. Note that Address Book images are displayed at a maximum of 88×88 pixels. If the image is smaller than that in both dimensions, it will be scaled up. If the image is longer in one dimension than in the other, then the longest dimension will be scaled to 88 pixels. If you want the best images in the Address Book, then you should scale the images down on the desktop so that they look good at 88 pixels. The Gimp (*http://www.gimp.org*) is a great program for doing this kind of manipulation.

You can copy over either JPEGs or Windows bitmaps. The location on the memory card is something like: */DCIM/<filename>.jpg* (or *.bmp*). If this path doesn't already exist on your expansion card, go ahead and create it and put your image files there. This should work on most devices. If it doesn't work on your device, try using the Image Converter (or related software such as Data Export) from the desktop to copy over some images. Then check your memory card to see where the images were stored.

Address Book

After you have loaded some pictures on to your Palm device, run Address Book. Tap on a name to add an image to it. Tap on Edit, and tap the words No Image (or the existing image if you want to replace it). This will bring up a pop-up menu that lets you remove the image from the address or choose a different image. From the image chooser, the images you transferred should be visible. Choose the one you want and it should appear.

H A C K #5 Get More Out of MemoPad

Write text and you're done—that's what MemoPad is about, right? Well, yes, in the same sense that music is just vibrations in the air. These hacks let you go beyond MemoPad's basic capabilities.

Because the standard applications have been fundamentally unchanged since the first Palm Pilot, they tend to be dismissed by power users. It is the standard applications' apparent simplicity that makes these hacks even more powerful.

As with the other standard applications, this hack is divided into a series of sections. The first two apply equally well to MemoPad and to the attached notes that are available in the other standard applications.

Phone Lookup

If you select text corresponding to an entry (or the prefix of one of the entries) in the Address Book, you can choose Phone Lookup from the Options menu to replace the selected text with the corresponding text from the Address Book. The prefix is whatever appears at the start of the line in the Address Book List view. For example, a company would match the company name. If you only have a first name for someone, then it would match the first name. Otherwise, the match will be on either the last name (if you are viewing last names first) or the company name followed by a comma and the last name (if you are viewing company names first). If the text you have selected matches more than one entry, then the Address Book List view will appear to let you choose the contact you want. The text that comes back is the same text that appears in the List view, except that it won't be abbreviated. Thus, whichever phone number or email address you had chosen to display [Hack #3] will get copied over when you select Phone Lookup. Note that you can select a single word in MemoPad by double-tapping it. This can make it easier to pick out a prefix to match for a lookup.

Capital Letters

Memos (and attached notes) automatically start with an uppercase letter, even if you write it as lowercase. This is great except for the rare occasions when you really do want to start with a lowercase letter. The easiest thing to do then is just to write the letter twice (the second appears in lowercase) and delete the one that comes out in uppercase.

You will also get the same behavior after entering a period. The next letter you enter will be converted to uppercase. This feature can be nice—you don't have to do anything special (e.g., draw the uppercase stroke in Graffiti or shift to the uppercase area in Graffiti 2) to capitalize these characters.

Writing Text

From the memo list you can start writing text to create a new memo. The memo will be created in the current category or in Unfiled if the current category is All (otherwise it will use the currently selected category). This is a nice shortcut that is available in some variant in the standard applications.

Cheap Spreadsheet

You can use MemoPad as a free spreadsheet, if all you need it for is simple layouts. You can use tabs and spaces to line up columns. For example, you can keep track of your accrued and used vacation with MemoPad.

You can also use MemoPad to keep track of your character in a role-playing game [Hack #18], as you can see in Figure 1-11. You can keep track of important stats, to-hit and damage modifiers, saving throw bonuses, and your current hit points and experience. You can also list your spells, skills, and equipment. You can list the page numbers of the corresponding sections in the player's guide next to each item.

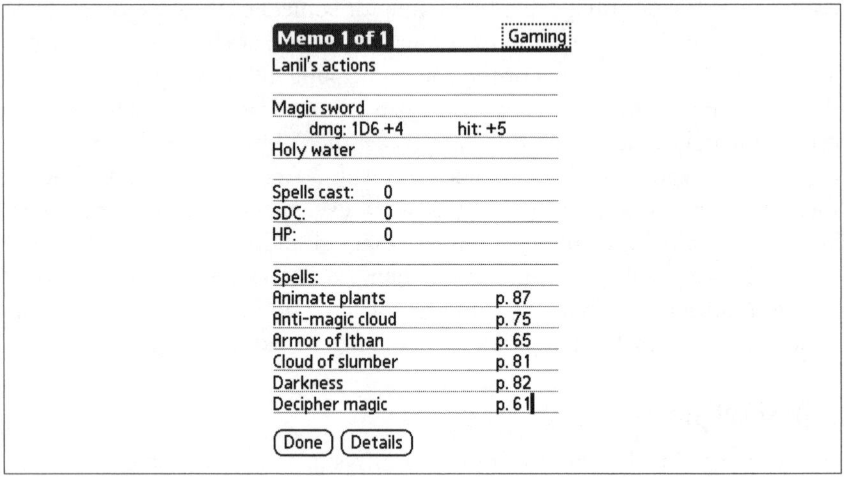

Figure 1-11. MemoPad as character sheet

Templates

Do you write a lot of notes that are very similar? If so, then you can use *templates*. Create a new category called Templates. Create skeleton memos that have all of the common structure and text. Name each one appropriately so you can distinguish them. When you want to use one of your templates, tap on it and use Select All and then Copy from the Edit menu. Tap New Memo from the Record menu and paste in the copied text. Set the category of the new memo, change its name, and fill out the skeleton.

Some devices support Appointment Templates directly. For example, in Treos and Visors, you can tap New to make a new appointment. You will be given an option to use a template. You can turn an existing appointment into a template by selecting the appointment and choosing Create Template from the menu.

See Also

- "Tweak Every Setting" [Hack #46]
- "Annotate Everything" [Hack #8]
- "Improve Text Entry" [Hack #24]

Show Palm Desktop Who's Boss

As with the standard Palm applications, the Palm desktop is a fairly simple program. Don't mistake this simplicity for inflexibility, though; you can usually get it to do what you want even when the solution is not obvious.

The desktop is powerful, if you know how to use it. You can use the desktop to restore a Palm device or PC. You can command different views of data. You can take charge of importing data to load addresses and contacts from a variety of sources. All this power is freely available in the desktop.

 If you sync with Microsoft Outlook instead of the Palm desktop, then you may not see anything in Palm desktop. Most modern Palm devices ship with Chapura PocketMirror. If you have enabled this conduit, then it will take over contacts, To Do's, and so on and you won't see anything in Palm desktop.

Reinstall Applications

If you need to reinstall applications and you don't have the *.prc* file anymore, then you have an alternative. Any applications that you have ever installed on your Palm device are stored in one of two locations: *c:\Program Files\Palm Handheld\<HotSync ID>\Archive* and *c:\Program Files\Palm Handheld\<HotSync ID>\Backup*. You can modify this directory when you first install the desktop software, so you may need to look around a bit. Also, for a Treo 600, the directory will have *Handspring* instead of *Palm Handheld*. Also notice that if you have a space in your HotSync ID, then the name will get modified (at least on Windows). For example, "Jeff Ishaq" becomes "IshaqJ."

Once you have figured out the path, you can simply point the Install tool at these locations and select the programs you want to reinstall. You will also need to install any necessary *.pdb* files and any related *.prc* files. For example, some applications require third-party *.pdb* or *.prc* files such as WABA or CASL. Applications that have been selected for installation but have not yet been copied over to the Palm device can be found in *c:\Program Files\Palm Handheld\<HotSync ID>\Install*.

Useful Views

Usually we think of the Palm desktop as a data entry tool or as an installation tool only. The Palm desktop can also be used as a data viewer. There are several views which can be useful.

In the Date Book, the Week and Month views can be helpful. The larger screen of a desktop machine (compared to a Palm device) allows much more information to be shown in these views. Thus, you will see not only which days have scheduled events, but you will also see the name of each event. These views give you a much better feel for the week and month than the Palm calendar.

> The Daily view also gives you a compound view of the To Do List or the Address Book, if you like.

The Address Book provides a Business Card view. This view gives you a nicely formatted picture of a number of entries simultaneously. Also, the Large Icon and Small Icon views add an icon to each entry which represents whether the entry is for a company or an individual. The algorithm is very simple. If an address has a company name but no first or last name, then it is considered to be a business. Any other combinations are treated as individuals.

HotSync Preferences

You can set the HotSync preferences for each of the built-in applications and any other conduits (see Figure 1-12). Select Custom from the HotSync menu to bring up a listing of conduits and the currently selected actions. Change the settings for a conduit by selecting it and hitting the Change button. Then, choose between *Synchronize the files* (takes the latest version from both the Palm device and the desktop), *Desktop overwrites handheld*, *Handheld overwrites Desktop*, and *Do nothing*. The overwrite options are useful if you need to update or repair a PC or Palm device.

The Change dialog box also has a checkbox called *Set as default*. If this is checked, then the selected action will become the default action for that conduit on every HotSync. If the box is not checked, then the selected action will only take effect for one HotSync, and then the default action will be restored. This makes sense for the overwrite options. If you are merely updating a PC or Palm device, then you probably don't want to use that action more than once.

View Deleted Items

Whenever you delete an item on your Palm device, you get a confirmation dialog box. This dialog box contains a checkbox labeled Save archive copy on PC. If you check this box, you can view deleted records using the Palm desktop application after doing a HotSync.

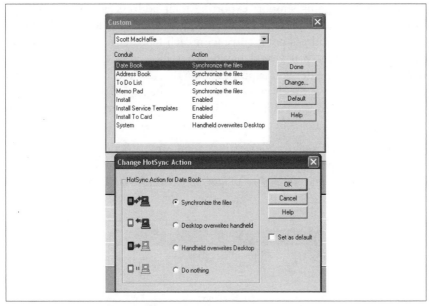

Figure 1-12. HotSync preferences in the Palm desktop

To view deleted records from the Palm desktop, you need to switch to the application (Date Book, Address Book, To Do List, or MemoPad) whose records you want to see. Next, select Open Archive from the File menu. You will need to select the appropriate archive file from the file browser that comes up. While you have an archive open for an application, the Palm desktop won't let you switch to another application. To switch back to live data (and regain the ability to switch applications), select Open Current from the File menu. You can also save the current data as an archive which you can open later with Open Archive. To save the current data, select Save All from the File menu.

Import Data

You can import data into the desktop in various formats. For general use, the most common interchange format is comma-separated value or CSV files. You can import CSV data into the Address Book or MemoPad. Of the two, the Address Book is the more useful. For either application, select Import from the File menu, then choose a *.csv* file from the browser. After that, you will be presented with a dialog box similar to Figure 1-13. You can match up Palm fields (on the left) with columns in the *.csv* file (on the right). You can rearrange the Palm fields to match the order in the *.csv* file by dragging the Palm fields up and down the list. You can also disable Palm fields that don't appear in the list by turning off the checkbox by the field name.

Many email programs support exporting their address books as *.csv* files. You can use this as a source for the Palm address book. One helpful tip is to create a dummy address book entry with each field set to the name of that field. For example, you would have entries like First, Last, email, Work phone, and so on. After you export the data to a *.csv* file, edit the file using a text editor and move the dummy record up to the top of the file. When you import this file into the Palm desktop, the dummy record will guide you in arranging the Palm fields in the correct order.

You can also use Excel to convert just about any program's exported data format to a properly formatted *.csv* file. Thus, you can export the data, import to Excel, and re-export to get something that Palm desktop can import.

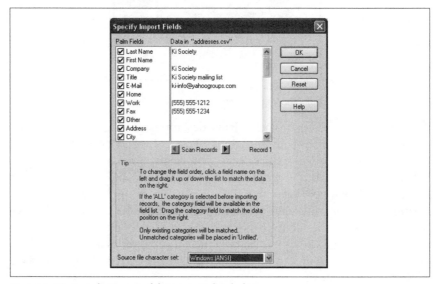

Figure 1-13. Sample import of data into Palm desktop

Use MemoPad as a Data Viewer

You can dump arbitrary text data into MemoPad using copy and paste, or you can import text files as memos. Then you can look at the data later on your Palm device. This data could be sales figures, text from a web site, your stock portfolio, programming references, or anything else you can think of. Memos are limited to 4,000 characters, though, so whatever it is, it has to be short. You can get replacement programs such as MegaMemo2 (*http://www. freewarepalm.com/utilities/megamemo2.shtml*) which allow you to have memos up to 32,767 characters. Also, some more recent devices such as the Zire 72 no longer have the 4K memo limit.

Find Anything

#7

Do you ever have trouble finding something on your PDA that you know is there? There are replacements for the Find tool which provide more flexibility in searching.

When you can't find what you're looking for, there are a couple of solutions. One possibility is to always add annotations to everything [Hack #8]. You can add notes to entries in the Date Book, Address Book, and To Do Lists. If you add a note to one of these items and do a search for words in the note, then Find will turn up the note. Then you can just click Done from the note and it will take you back to the related item. However, if you haven't been adding notes to everything as you go or you can't remember enough of the notes to search effectively, you need stronger medicine.

There are several replacement Find tools that have more flexibility than the built-in Find tool.

BeiksFind

This application allows you to find a string anywhere within a word, rather than having to match complete words. This can be useful if you remember the last few digits of a phone number, for example. You can find it at *http://www.beiks.com*.

FindHack

Despite the name, FindHack is a standalone application, not a HackMaster hack. This application allows you to select which databases and applications to search. Also, it does partial matching, supports wildcards, and allows for Boolean searching for complex criteria, as you can see in Figure 1-14. This works on Palm OS versions from 3.3 through 5.x. You can find this hack at *http://perso.wanadoo.fr/fpillet*.

superFinderHack

superFinderHack provides more flexibility in searching. It remembers the last 128 searches that you've done. Also, you can set the order that applications are searched in. Unlike FindHack, this actually is a HackMaster extension [Hack #47], so you will need to have HackMaster (or a replacement) installed. This hack only works on Palm OS versions from 3.1-4.x. You can find it at *http://home.columbus.rr.com/nevai/palm*.

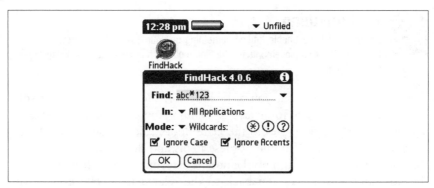

Figure 1-14. FindHack

Use Wildcards

The wildcard features in these replacements can be very powerful. For example, you can search for H*Master to find references to HackMaster, Hit-Master, or similar strings. You can search for phone numbers with a particular prefix by searching for something like: 555-????. The question marks match a single character—in this case, matching four digits for a phone number.

H A C K
#8   Annotate Everything

Do you ever have trouble remembering what To Do items or addresses mean on your PDA? Here are some tips that will make sure that never happens again.

It is easy to jot down a phone number or give yourself an item to do without including enough information to understand it later. Using the annotation tools (notes for To Do items, notes and custom fields for addresses) can eliminate this problem, if you annotate well. Here are the built-in Palm applications that can be annotated:

Address Book
    Open a contact, then tap Details → Note.

Date Book
    Open an appointment, then tap Details → Note.

Expense
    Tap an expense to select it, then tap Details → Note.

To Do List
    Tap an item to select it, then tap Details → Note.

Why?

The most important question to ask is why. Why are you writing down this phone number? Why do you need this To Do item? If you can articulate why, then add the reason as an annotation. You can also ask why again to dig deeper for the underlying reason. When you find the underlying reason, then you can add that as another annotation. For an example of additional details for an address, see Figure 1-15.

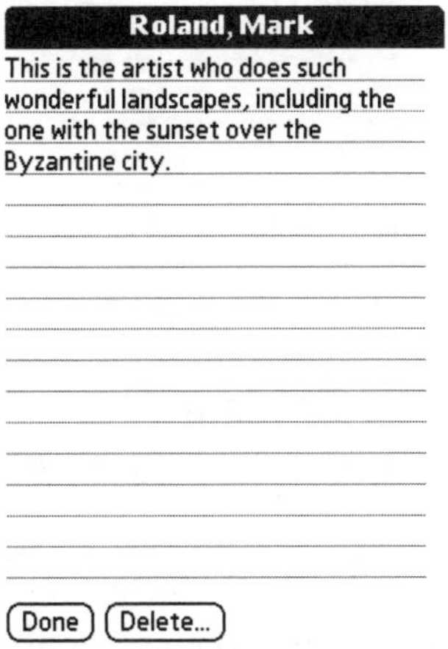

Figure 1-15. Additional information for an address

How?

Describing how you are going to accomplish your To Do items is another useful type of annotation. For example, if your To Do item is to bake a cake, then the annotation might list the recipe. This is useful if you have an idea about how to do something—capture it so that the idea will be handy when you start in on your task.

Try to think about how long you will need to remember this information. If you are jotting down tasks for today, then you may not need a lot of explanation. If you are planning things months in advance, however, then you may need to put more detail into the annotations so that you remember exactly what you need to do when the time comes. You can see an example in Figure 1-16.

These ideas should get you started, but remember that annotations need to be useful to you. It is easy to add items to your Palm device without thinking ahead. A little bit of planning and adding an annotation can save you a lot of time later when you are trying to figure out what you meant.

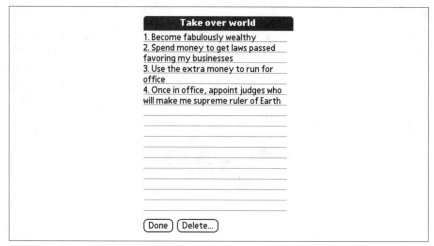

Take over world

1. Become fabulously wealthy
2. Spend money to get laws passed favoring my businesses
3. Use the extra money to run for office
4. Once in office, appoint judges who will make me supreme ruler of Earth

(Done) (Delete...)

Figure 1-16. To Do List showing how to accomplish a task

HACK #9 Become a Better Student

Use your Palm device to help you keep track of assignments and organize your time to become a better student.

Palm Powered handhelds can be extremely helpful for students because they allow you to carry all of your important personal information, as well as electronic references and e-books, in the palm of your hand. But unless you know the right tricks, you may not be using your handheld to its fullest potential. Whether you're a high school, college, or graduate student, you can use your handheld to keep track of all of the information relating to your classes, ensure that you never turn in a late paper, and even get higher grades.

First, enter all of the relevant information into your handheld on the first day of class. Many teachers and professors hand out course information sheets or a syllabus on the first day, and many students put them in a folder or notebook immediately and don't pay much attention to them. But this is the time to enter all of that information into your Palm Powered handheld, and you should capture everything you can:

- Go ahead and block out time for every class meeting by creating a repeating meeting in the Date Book [Hack #1].

- Is there any contact information listed for the teacher or professor? At the college and graduate levels, you should expect to find a phone number, email address, office location, and the times the professor is available for office hours. Go ahead and add the relevant information to the

Address Book and put the extra information such as office hours in the note for that entry.

- Are there any important due dates like papers, presentations, or tests? Go ahead and add those to your calendar as well. You might also want to consider adding an alarm for a few days beforehand to remind you of the event—and to make sure you don't have to stay up all night studying for a test because you forgot it was coming up.

- Will you have to purchase any textbooks or reading packets? Add an entry to your To Do List reminding you to purchase them now; otherwise you may find that the books are sold out at the campus bookstore. Go ahead and make a To Do category for each class because you'll be entering in more detailed information about your assignments as well.

Second, take all of your relevant class notes using your Palm OS handheld and an accessory keyboard, if possible. If you're in high school, computers and handheld devices may not be allowed in the classroom, but college students should definitely be able to do this. This is helpful for several reasons, and can save plenty of time when you need to review and prepare for exams at the end of the semester:

- All of your notes will be backed up when you synchronize your device, so you'll never have to worry about losing all of your work if a (paper) notebook is misplaced.

- Your notes will also be instantly searchable on both your handheld and on the computer, so if you need to look up a particular term, everything is right there and quickly accessible.

- You also won't have any worries about trying to decipher quickly scribbled notes when you're reviewing several weeks later. Even better, if you're a relatively quick typist you can capture all of the information you need more quickly than writing, so that you're free to focus more of your attention on the teacher and the lecture, instead of frantically trying to get everything down.

You can use the built in Memo Pad for this, or your device may have come with a word processing program such as Documents to Go or WordSmith. There are replacement programs for Memo Pad available, such as MegaMemo2 (*http://www.freewarepalm.com/utilities/megamemo2.shtml*), which allow you to have memos of 32K characters instead of 4K. No matter what program you use, the key is to ensure that it synchronizes with your computer so that you can back up and search your notes. You won't need any paper in class, unless the subject you're studying requires a good amount of drawing, charts, or graphs. There are several drawing programs available for Palm OS handhelds, but pen and paper are easier to use in a classroom setting.

Third, develop a regular study schedule. You can block out time in the Date Book for regular daily and weekly study, and it's also a good idea to enter in all of the reading assignments that will be covered in each class period. You'll be prepared for every class, and won't have to worry about trying to "hide" in the back of the class so the professor won't call on you. Regular review is also the key to effective test preparation; staying up all night before an exam can leave you too tired to answer the questions and write good essays. You'll likely forget everything you crammed into your brain as soon as the test is over, which won't provide a very good foundation for additional study.

Instead, take a look at what each test will cover and break the material down into smaller parts. You can then create To Dos in your Palm Powered handheld that remind you to go over a certain section in your notes or read a chapter in your textbook. And if you have a fear of writing papers and essays, as many students do, you can break that large task down into several incremental goals that are easier to accomplish. If you have to write a ten page paper on the history of the Civil War, for example, you'll need to do some research, develop a thesis, block out some time to write and edit the paper, prepare a bibliography, and so on. Each one of those tasks can either be scheduled for a particular time on your calendar (if you suffer from procrastination, as so many students do!) or as a To Do item that can be checked off of your list when completed. By following a plan for writing your paper that provides plenty of time for preparation, you'll end up with a superior finished product, less stress, and hopefully higher grades.

You may also want to consider purchasing more specialized software and resources to get the most use out of your handheld in an educational context. Some of my favorite applications and strategies are listed here.

Agendus

Agendus (*http://www.iambic.com/agendus/palmos/*) is a full featured PIM replacement that integrates the Date Book, Address, To Do, and Memo functions built into your Palm Powered handheld. Besides offering color coding, icons, and a variety of views for your data, it also adds a Contact Linking feature that is very powerful. Create a contact for each of your classes in a special category, such as English, History, Calculus, Physics, Spanish, and so on and then link that contact to each of the relevant pieces of information about that class—exams, due dates for papers, reading assignments, and so forth. You can then use the Contact History function to find everything related to that class at a moment's notice. You can also add icons and color and use the monthly calendar to see which weeks are going to be the busiest so that you can plan ahead and perhaps do a few reading assignments early for one class so you'll have time to prepare for an exam in another.

ShadowPlan

Notes taken in outline form are generally more organized and easier to review at a later date. One of the most powerful outlining applications available for Palm OS devices is ShadowPlan from Code Jedi (*http://www.codejedi.com*). You can create any number of outlines and also link individual items on those outlines to the built-in applications.

There are a variety of course management applications especially designed for students, such as 4.0 Student, CoursePro, Due Yesterday, and Thought-Manager for Students. You can find more information and links to all of them in the PalmSource How-To Guide for Students, located at: *http://www.palmsource.com/interests/education_student/*.

—Jen Edwards

HACK #10 Keep Track of Your Collectibles

If you are a collector, you can use MemoPad or a specialized utility to manage your hobby.

If you're a collector of anything from books to Precious Moments figurines, you may have a hard time keeping track of what you have in your collection and what you still need to acquire. Fortunately this task can be greatly simplified with a Palm Powered handheld. You can keep it simple and use a variety of Memo Pad entries, or you can use a more specialized application to track everything from what you have in your collection to how much you paid for it and an estimation of current value.

MemoPad

If you have a relatively small or uncomplicated collection, you may find that the built-in MemoPad is all you need to keep things under control. You can have up to 15 categories of memos, so you can create a separate category for each collection or you can have one *Collectibles* category. You can then use individual MemoPad entries for groups of items, say books by the same author, or Hallmark ornaments organized by year. This method isn't going to work for an incredibly large collection, but if you just want to make sure you don't purchase duplicate DVDs, this is a good method to use. Even better, when you get information about something you want to purchase you can add the relevant information to the MemoPad, so the next time you're shopping you'll have everything you need to make the best addition to your collection. MemoPad replacements, such as pedit (*http://www.paulcomputing.com*), allow you to sort the lines in a memo (see Figure 1-17), which can be useful if you have a lot of items listed.

p04 #1 of 1　　　　　　　　Unfiled

Star Wars

line sorter	ⓘ

# of skipped fields:　　　**0**

+ # of skipped columns:　**0**

# of compared columns:　**0**

☐ ignore case　☐ skip lead blanks

Alphabetic　Numerical

Reverse　.Cancel　Forward

Figure 1-17. Sorting in pedit

ShadowPlan

Shadow Plan is an outliner, but it also does a very good job of handling lists of all kinds. I've found that the best method is to start a new outline for each kind of collectible, such as DVDs, books, or hub caps. Within the outline, create top level *parent items* for each category; the screenshot (Figure 1-18) shows the sample setup for a book collection. I have a rather extensive book collection, so I chose to organize the list by topic; under each topic I've listed books by title, or when I have several by the same author, by author as sub-topic with the individual titles listed below. I can attach a note to any or all of the items that contains additional information such as the condition of the book, the publisher, the price, notes from my reading, and so on. I also use Shadow's tagging feature to locate the book on a particular shelf, which makes finding any book in my collection very simple.

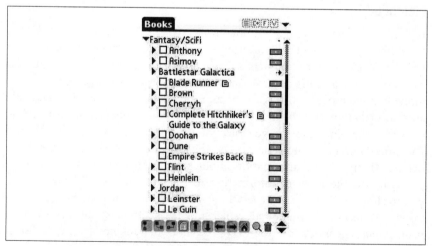

Figure 1-18. Using ShadowPlan to track books

This setup could be adapted to suit any sort of collection, from the most mundane to the most elaborate. Within each outline you can set up areas for what items you have or are looking for, as well as information about dealers and shops that carry the sort of collectible that interests you. ShadowPlan has many other uses, as well as a very active online discussion group. For more information about ShadowPlan, visit the Code Jedi web site at *http:// www.codejedi.com*.

HandyShopper

This is an unusual recommendation based on one of the most popular Palm OS applications ever. HandyShopper is a freeware grocery shopping manager, but beneath that simple interface is a surprisingly powerful database. It requires a bit of tweaking to set up correctly, especially since you'll be using it for something slightly different than what it was designed for. But with some careful thought and planning, you can turn HandyShopper into a rather powerful database application. You can start by creating a different shopping list for each type of collectible, and then using "stores" to organize your collectibles. If you have a large movie collection, you could have stores like Comedy, Drama, Fantasy, Horror, and Romance, with a list of items contained within each store. Each item can have its own notes, and since HandyShopper is designed to handle shopping tasks, it already has built-in fields for quantity and price. There are also some desktop applications available that allow HandyShopper lists to be imported from and exported to Microsoft Excel. You can get a free copy of HandyShopper from PalmGear at *http://www.palmgear.com*. Also, be sure to check out the very active discussion group at *http://groups.yahoo.com/group/handyshopper/*.

Database

For the truly serious collector, a database application is the best option. Since databases are customizable, you can add all of the fields you need to adequately describe your collectibles. Example fields include:

- Item Name
- Date Acquired
- Purchase Price
- Purchased From
- Current Value
- Date Sold
- Selling Price
- Notes—variations, etc.

One of my personal favorites is Piranha from FPS Software. It's very easy to use and has a robust Windows desktop companion application available that quickly and easily imports and exports databases to Microsoft Excel. You can get a free trial at *http://www.fps.com*. A more advanced option is HanDBase from DDH Software; it has a desktop application capable of communicating with Microsoft Access but has a much steeper learning curve. You can learn more at *http://www.ddhsoftware.com/*.

Conclusion

With the right inventory system, you can easily keep track of all of your collectibles, whether you have 5 porcelain dolls, 75 DVDs, or 500 Hallmark Christmas ornaments.

—Jen Edwards

## CHAPTER TWO

Palm Applications
Hacks 11–17

This chapter covers creative uses for applications. Some of these hacks cover specific uses for both the built-in applications and third-party applications. Other hacks cover novel uses for third-party applications only. These hacks provide detailed instructions and advice for the given tasks. Even if you aren't interested in a particular task, you might still find some useful information to apply to something you are interested in.

There are thousands of applications available for Palm OS. PalmGear lists more than 20,000 applications. A few hacks can't even give a good overview of all the applications that are available. Rather than attempting that, these hacks go into more detail in limited areas.

Although the built-in applications are very useful and can be made to fit a variety of tasks, sometimes specialized applications are a better choice. Some of the third-party applications are general tools and some are specific to a certain task.

HACK #11 Manage Projects

You can use a Palm device to help you manage complicated projects with resources and dependencies, such as a software development project.

Projects come in different complexities. Before choosing a tool to help manage your project, you need to consider the complexity of the project you want to manage. Different tools are better for different levels of complexity.

Project management software represents the world as tasks, resources, and dependencies between tasks. Although all project management software has a common view of the world, each package differs in how it lets you arrange things. So, when you pick a software package, you need to consider factors such as:

How many tasks need to be managed?
More tasks make a project more complex.

Can the tasks be grouped into higher-level tasks?
Hierarchical tasks make projects more complex.

Are there dependencies to consider?
Complicated dependencies push a project into the complex category.

Is there a strict ordering of tasks, or can the tasks be freely rearranged?
Being able to freely rearrange tasks is a sign of a simple project.

Do you need to track people and assignments as well as tasks?
More items (such as budget, equipment, or other resources) to track make for a more complex project.

How frequently will the tasks or dependencies change?
If there is likely to be a lot of change, then a simpler project is better.

Simple Projects

A simple project has few dependencies and doesn't require a strict ordering of tasks. A simple project also doesn't require tight scheduling of the people working on the project.

On the other hand, simple projects can deal with hierarchical tasks and are good for managing change—rearranging, adding, and deleting tasks.

You may be able to use the built-in To Do List [Hack #2] to manage simple projects, as seen in Figure 2-1. You can set priorities on items and assign due dates to individual items. These will be reflected in the Today view of the Date Book (on recent Palm devices) or the Today view in FacerLauncher [Hack #45]. You can even use the categories to group individual tasks into larger tasks.

However, the To Do List doesn't have any way of tracking effort, time spent (such as hours or days), or estimates against the actual time spent. Also, there isn't an easy way to get an overall look at the project and how far along it is.

A better way of managing simple projects is to use a spreadsheet such as MiniCalc [Hack #14]. The spreadsheet only needs a few columns: the name of the task, estimated effort, remaining effort, and optionally, the name of the person assigned to the task. Larger tasks can be created as the sum of lower-level tasks as you can see in the screenshot of MiniCalc in Figure 2-2. The advantage of using a spreadsheet over the To Do List is that you can see how

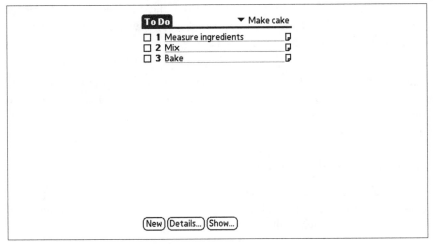

Figure 2-1. Managing a simple project with the To Do List

the project is doing at any moment. You can write simple formulas to track progress. With the "remaining" column, you can make estimates of how long the remaining tasks will take to complete.

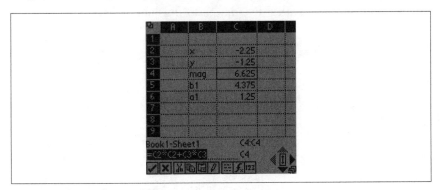

Figure 2-2. MiniCalc spreadsheet

Binary Tracking

Binary tracking is a technique for preventing the "90% done" syndrome. Projects can be 90% complete for a long time. I saw a project that was 90% complete for over a year, despite being actively worked on the entire time.

Binary tracking simply holds that each low-level task can be either 100% complete or 0%—no in-between numbers are allowed. Then, higher-level tasks can be computed as the sum of the completed lower-level tasks weighted by their duration.

Here is a simple example: if you have ten one-day low-level tasks that form one high-level task, then each completed (100%) low-level task adds 10% to the high-level task's completion.

Not only does this make estimation easier and more accurate, but it provides another benefit for software development. In developing software, if you have nine features that are 100% complete, you may be able to ship the product. On the other hand, if you have ten features that are all 90% done, then you can't ship.

Moderately Complex Projects

Moderately complex projects require you to view the status of the project broken down by tasks and sub-tasks. It may also be important to filter tasks by various criteria such as due date.

Moderately complex projects can be managed with a list or task manager. ShadowPlan (*http://www.codejedi.com*) is a good example of a task manager. You can use it to create hierarchical tasks as in Figure 2-3. The parent tasks' completion percentages are calculated automatically from their children. Unfortunately, all children are weighted equally. Thus, if you have a one-day task grouped with a five-day task, finishing either of them marks the parent as being 50% complete.

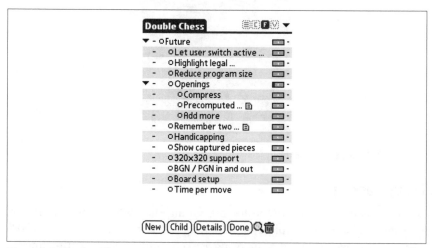

Figure 2-3. ShadowPlan as a project management tool

ShadowPlan allows you to assign start, target, and finish dates for tasks, and it has sophisticated filters for viewing items. Other list and task managers have similar capabilities.

Complex Projects

Complex projects require the most support. They may require dependencies, or they may require careful allocation of people or resources. They may need to have a strict ordering of tasks. It may be necessary to view dependencies, estimated and actual completion dates, resource usage, and milestones.

Complex projects need real project management software. One open-source application is called Progect (*http://sourceforge.net/projects/progect/*), seen in Figure 2-4. There is an application called Project@Hand (*http://www.natara.com/*) that allows you to synchronize with Microsoft Project. You can view and modify projects on your handheld. The same company makes a product called Project@Hand2 which is a standalone project management application for the Palm. Another full-featured project management application for Palm is FastTrack Schedule (*http://www.aecsoftware.com*), seen in Figure 2-5. You can also use a list manager or outliner, such as Thought-Manager (*http://www.handshigh.com/*).

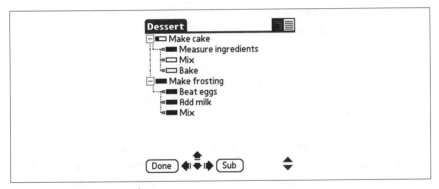

Figure 2-4. Progect screenshot

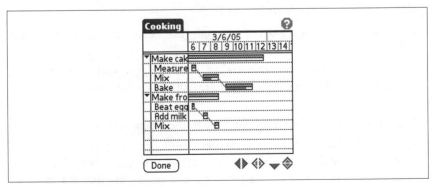

Figure 2-5. FastTrack Schedule

One thing that project management software lacks is the ability to handle change easily. If some tasks get completed out of order, it can be very difficult to go back and update the project data to reflect the new task order.

Instructions

This discussion uses a simple task example to walk through how to use the various types of programs. An example task is shown in Table 2-1. Note that the columns are task name, time in minutes, and person.

Table 2-1. Example tasks

Main task	Sub-task	Time	Person
Make cake			
	Measure ingredients	10	John
	Mix	20	John
	Bake	30	John
Make frosting			
	Beat eggs	5	Susan
	Add milk	5	Susan
	Mix	5	Susan

To start, you need to download an appropriate spreadsheet or project management application or just use the To Do application. Then use the following instructions.

Spreadsheet. A spreadsheet is a good choice for a simple to moderately complex project (see Figure 2-6). Once the project gets complex enough to require more than two screenfuls of information, you should look to a more sophisticated tool. Here's how you can set up the sample project in Mini-Calc (*http://www.solutionsinhand.com*):

1. Create column headings: Task, Sub-task, Estimate, Remaining, and Person.

2. Lay out the tasks and estimates. All estimates should be in the same units—typically days or weeks. Enter all of the data from the example task.

3. For each line, set the remaining time to the estimated time.

4. For the higher-level tasks, set the estimated times equal to the sum of the times for the lower-level tasks. For MakeCake, that would be something like =sum(c3:c5). You can copy and paste that formula from the

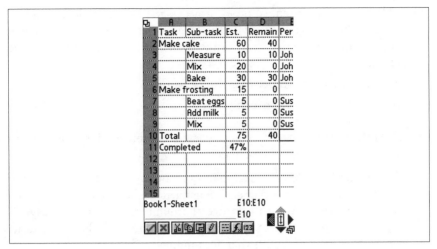

Figure 2-6. MiniCalc displaying a spreadsheet for a simple project

estimated column to the remaining column. The spreadsheet will automatically switch the formula to be =sum(d3:d5). Do the same for the frosting task.

5. Create a Total line that sums up the estimated and remaining times. For estimated time, the formula will be something like =sum(c3:c5,c7:c9). You can then copy and paste it into the Remaining column and the spreadsheet will adjust the formula for you.

6. Create a Percentage complete cell. The formula is something like =(c8-b8)/c8. Switch the cell's formatting to percentage.

7. As the lower-level tasks get finished, set the Remaining cells to 0. You should see the related numbers (higher-level task, total, and percentage complete) update.

For higher-level tasks, you may want to set the background color to something different like light blue. You can also create total and completed lines for each person if you want.

To Do List. The To Do List is fine for the simplest of projects (refer back to Figure 2-1). Here's how you can set up the sample project:

1. Create two categories for the high-level tasks: *Make cake* and *Make frosting*.

2. Create one-line tasks for each of the low-level tasks in the appropriate categories.

3. Add more details in linked notes, if necessary. For example, you might include a list of ingredients with the *Measure ingredients* task. Also, you might include the temperature of the oven and how long to bake in the *Bake* task.

4. Prioritize tasks in the order they will be worked on.

5. Check tasks off as they are completed.

Project management software. If you're using a comprehensive project management suite, there's more you can do:

1. On the desktop side (if your application supports it, otherwise, on the Palm), set up tasks, people, and dependencies between tasks. For the example, you may want to change the numbers to: 1 day, 2 days, 3 days, and 0.5 days. Project management software works better for tasks measured in days and hours than for minutes.

2. Account for vacations, holidays, weekends, and any other non-productive time.

3. If necessary, apply a scaling factor (perhaps 80%) to people's ability to complete tasks.

4. Use your Palm to update tasks as they are completed, make changes, and keep an eye on tasks.

Each of these project styles has its own requirements and solutions. You should pick a tool that matches the kind of project you are managing.

HACK #12   Lose Weight the Palm Way

The best way to lose weight is to count calories and exercise regularly, while tracking your progress. Your Palm device can make this easier.

If you simply eat less food, your body will adjust by slowing your metabolism. The best way to counteract this slowing is to increase your exercise at the same time you are decreasing your calories.

Tracking all of this information is complex. How many calories were in that donut you had for a snack? How many calories do you burn while walking a mile? And if you successfully lose weight, how does that affect the calories you burn during exercise?

Calorie and Exercise Counters

There are applications such as BalanceLog (*http://www.healthetech.com*) that can manage this information for you. BalanceLog contains lists of foods and exercises and the related calorie amounts. You can see a summary in Figure 2-7. For exercise, the calories burned per hour is adjusted by your weight. As you lose weight, you burn fewer calories. Having a program on your Palm device to track this is nice because you usually have your Palm device with you. Thus, you can enter meals and exercise in a timely fashion, instead of entering them when you get home and having to remember back over the day.

My Daily Calorie Budget: 2170
Calories I've eaten today: 0
Balance (Under Budget): 2170
Exercise Calories Burned: 0
I can eat 2170 more Calories today and still meet my goal.
Yesterday's Balance (Under): 2170
Cumulative Balance (Under): 4340

| Day | Week | Month |

3/6/05

Figure 2-7. Daily summary in BalanceLog

Sustained weight loss only comes with regular attention to the details—food and exercise. As always, check with a doctor before starting an exercise program or altering your diet.

Another program for tracking calories and exercise is EatWatch (*http://www. fourmilab.ch/hackdiet/palm/*). EatWatch (Figure 2-8) is designed to help you follow the Hacker's Diet. The Hacker's Diet is a combination of reducing your calories and doing some calisthenics. EatWatch helps you on both these counts. It tracks your food intake and the number of exercises that you do. The exercises include sit-ups, push-ups, jumping jacks, running in place, and a few more. You can find more about the Hacker's Diet at the Eat-Watch web page.

Info on the Go

You can carry nutrition information with you on your Palm device. Memoware (*http://www.memoware.com*) has a number of documents in its Food and Nutrition area. You need a document reader [Hack #23] to view these documents. The information includes general nutrition information as well as specific types of information such as low-carb foods or the glycemic indices of different foods. The glycemic index indicates how quickly your body converts the food to glucose, which is important for people with diabetes. A low glycemic number means that it takes the body longer to convert the food to glucose.

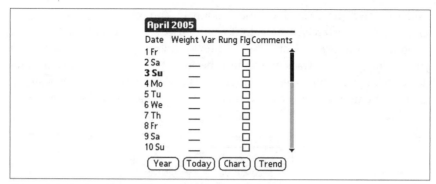

Figure 2-8. EatWatch, monthly view

Entertainment on the Go

You can also use your Palm device to listen to music [Hack #25] while you exercise. Portability makes a Palm device that much more useful for exercising. Pick out some good music, a decent music player, and some headphones that will work while you are exercising, and you are set. If you are going to be fairly stationary while you exercise, you could get some Bluetooth wireless headphones and leave your Palm device in your bag playing music. Otherwise, you will need to get a good sports case for your Palm device so that it can go with you without getting in the way of your exercise. You can find cases at Palm (*http://www.palm.com*) and most major electronics stores. Also, the Gadgeteer (*http://www.the-gadgeteer.com*) has reviews of just about every case ever produced for Palm devices.

Use the Built-in Applications

You can use the built-in applications to help with your weight-loss plans. Use the Date Book to schedule time for exercise. Or if you want to be a little less structured (maybe you want to go for a hike sometime during the weekend), then you can create a To Do item instead. For the hike, you could set a due date at the end of the weekend and check off the item in the To Do List when you finally head out, as you can see in Figure 2-9.

Eating right is a big part of losing weight. The built-in applications can help with cooking. You can use the To Do List to set up shopping lists, as in Figure 2-10. MemoPad makes a simple alternative to a full-fledged cooking program for organizing recipes, as you can see in Figure 2-11.

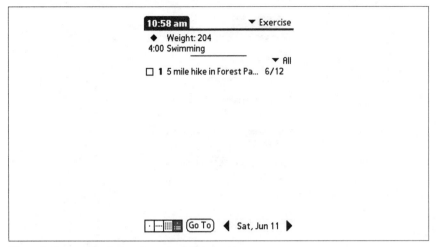

Figure 2-9. Date Book showing scheduled exercises

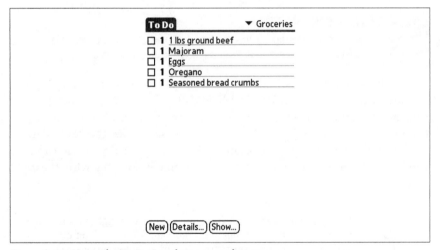

Figure 2-10. Using the To Do List for grocery shopping

If you don't want to buy an extra program to track your weight, then just create an untimed entry in the Date Book [Hack #1] each day that you weigh yourself and record your weight there. If you like pretty pictures, you can record your weight in a spreadsheet—date in one column, weight in another—and then graph the results to see your weight loss over time.

Losing weight takes patience and self-discipline. Your Palm device can make the process easier, but ultimately it's up to you to see it through.

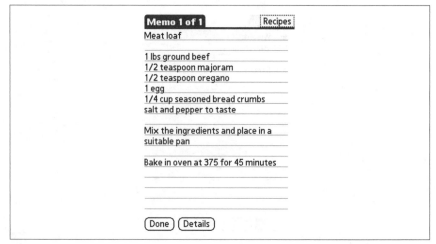

Figure 2-11. MemoPad showing a recipe

 HACK #13 # Watch the Stars

You are outside looking up at the stars, and you start to wonder what constellations you can see. Your Palm can help you identify the stars.

Your Palm has a couple of advantages over a traditional paper star guide. You are likely to have your Palm with you all the time. You probably won't have a star guide with you unless you are planning to observe the sky. A Palm device has a backlight, which makes it easier to see the constellations on the screen and read any associated text. Finally, a Palm device can help you manually aim your telescope or even aim it for you with the right accessories.

> Because white light can cause you to lose your night vision, you should affix a red film over your Palm screen to filter out the troublesome wavelengths. For more information, see *Astronomy Hacks* (O'Reilly, 2005). Some of the astronomy programs have a night mode that converts all of the white text and graphics to red.

There are several astronomy programs available.

Astro Info

Astro Info (*http://astroinfo.sourceforge.net*), seen in Figure 2-12, is an open-source astronomy program. It displays information and a small picture for each of the planets and the moon. It also comes with several star catalogs that you can use to view different stars and galaxies. There is also a night mode, which changes to red text on a black background. Night mode only works on 256 color Palms, though. It doesn't work on recent Palms with 64K colors.

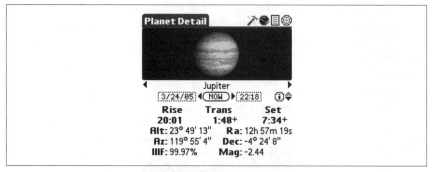

Figure 2-12. Astro Info screenshot showing Jupiter's details

Astromist

Astromist (http://www.astromist.com) is a full-featured astronomy tool. It includes star and planet charts (see Figure 2-13), high-resolution graphics, and support for controlling telescopes via hand controls or Bluetooth. You can look at sky views, including rotating and zooming views. Astromist includes a catalog of 2.5 million stars and 18,200 deep sky objects. Astromist also has special tools for Jupiter (red spot, satellites) and for the moon.

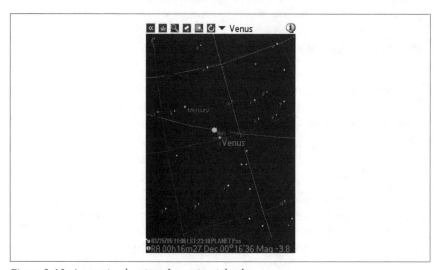

Figure 2-13. Astromist showing planets in night sky

Planetarium

Planetarium (*http://www.aho.ch/pilotplanets/*) can draw sky maps showing constellations, as seen in Figure 2-14. You can use Planetarium to locate stars or planets in the sky. Planetarium has a night mode that turns the text and graphics red to preserve your night vision. Also, Planetarium can control a telescope via the serial port, or you can read off the Az/Alt or RA/Dec coordinates to manually set up a telescope. For an in-depth look at Planetarium, see *Astronomy Hacks* (O'Reilly, 2005).

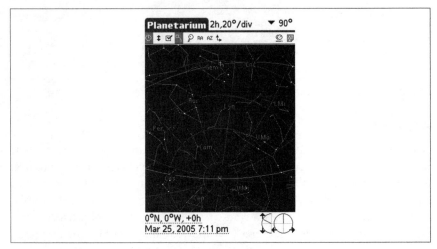

Figure 2-14. Planetarium sky map showing constellations

Astronomy Guide Pocket Directory Database

The Astronomy Guide (*http://www.pocketdirectory.com*) contains facts about celestial objects, including the planets. It also has some nice pictures. The Astronomy Guide is a database for the DataViewer program, which is included in the download. You can see an example of a picture of Jupiter in Figure 2-15.

Star Pilot Platinum

Star Pilot Platinum (*http://www.star-pilot.com*) is actually a collection of astronomy programs. Star Pilot is the main program. It can plot star and planet positions, as seen in Figure 2-16. It can also display the constellations on a star map. It supports high-resolution displays.

Hopefully these programs will help with your astronomy hobby or spark a new interest. Telescopes are good for hackers—you can even build your own or figure out how to control a commercial one with your Palm.

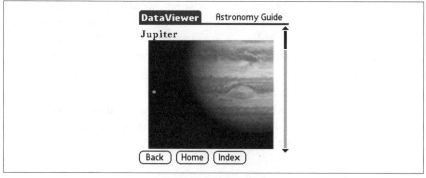

Figure 2-15. Jupiter displayed in the Astronomy Guide Pocket Directory Database

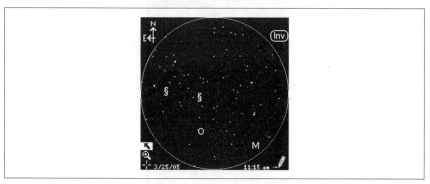

Figure 2-16. Star Pilot sky view

 ## HACK #14 Get Creative with a Spreadsheet

A spreadsheet is a useful tool—a hack in its own right. Spreadsheets can function as calculators, list managers, web layout tools, and more.

If you are going to make heavy use of a spreadsheet on your Palm, then it has to be easy to use. You need to be able to enter formulas and cells efficiently. Also, you need to be able to manage multiple spreadsheets and easily move between them.

There are several popular spreadsheets on the market:

Documents-to-Go
> DataViz's Documents-to-Go (*http://www.dataviz.com/*) is an office suite that is bundled with many Palms. It lets you edit Excel spreadsheets and convert them to a lightweight format for quick editing on the go.

QuickOffice
> The QuickOffice (*http://www.quickoffice.com/*) suite, like Documents-to-Go, offers Excel compatibility in a compact form. QuickOffice allows

you to work with native Excel spreadsheets without requiring a conduit to strip them down to a simpler format. This allows you to work with a spreadsheet on your Palm device and then beam or email it to a coworker's desktop computer, where the spreadsheet can be opened in its full glory in Excel.

MiniCalc

MiniCalc (*http://www.solutionsinhand.com*) is a standard spreadsheet. It allows you to resize columns, change the formatting (both numeric and colors), and add a number of functions to your formulas, as you can see in Figure 2-17.

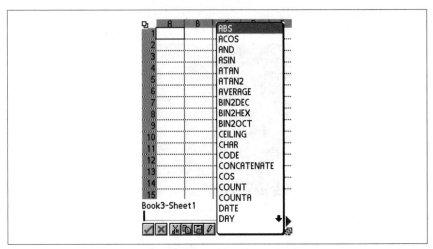

Figure 2-17. MiniCalc showing some of the available functions

TinySheet

TinySheet (*http://www.iambic.com*) includes a number of functions, organized by category. This is an improvement on MiniCalc which just gives you a single list containing all of the available functions. Tiny-Sheet provides control over formatting including colors and numeric formats.

Once you have installed a spreadsheet, what can you do with it? A spreadsheet is a tool, not an end result in itself. You can use a spreadsheet to manage a project [Hack #11] or for many other purposes.

Calculator

You can use a spreadsheet as a calculator—that's what it is, in effect. You can enter in simple arithmetic or complex expressions. Do you have trouble remembering what all the variables represent in financial calculations? Are you trying to figure out when your mortgage will be paid off? You can put names in one column (e.g., Loan amount, Interest, Additional payments), and you only have to set up the formula once. Whenever you need to make a change, the names will guide you. For example, you could use a spreadsheet as a handy retirement calculator, as in Figure 2-18.

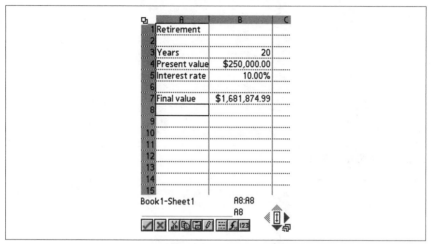

Figure 2-18. MiniCalc as a financial calculator

Web Layout

You can use a spreadsheet to help lay out web sites. You can block out areas of the screen using text and different colors. Save space for the banner at the top of the page by turning the first row's background color to blue. You can block out the navigation bar by changing the left column's background to red. Using colors to block out areas, together with a one- or two-word label (e.g., Banner, Navigation, Main Content) can help you to see the overall layout without getting bogged down in low-level details like font choices, as you can see in Figure 2-19. This works especially well if you are designing web pages for mobile devices.

List Manager

Using a spreadsheet as a list manager is easy. Put one item per line. As you complete items, you can change the background color of the row to something else—gray or green, perhaps. Or you can highlight uncompleted items with a yellow background to draw your eye, and then change back to white as the items are completed, as you can see in Figure 2-20.

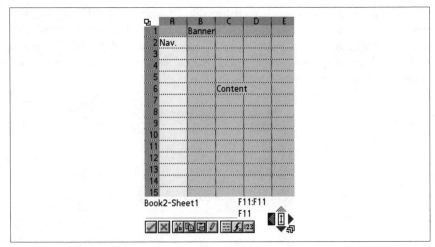

Figure 2-19. Spreadsheet as a web layout tool

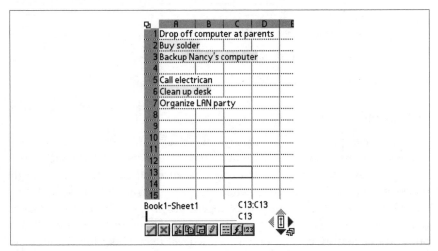

Figure 2-20. Spreadsheet as a list manager

Write Poetry

Some forms of poetry (e.g., poems by e.e. cummings) have a spatial component. You can play with this in a spreadsheet by dropping words or phrases into different cells. You can combine this with changing the background colors of cells to tweak the nose of your creativity. An example of writing a poem using a spreadsheet is in Figure 2-21.

As you can see, there are many uses for a spreadsheet. Think about it and see what other uses you can come up with.

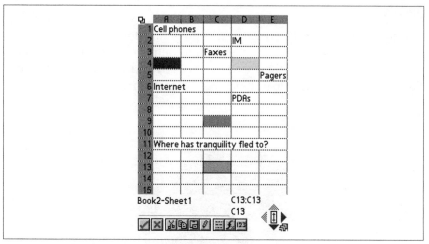

Figure 2-21. Writing a poem in a spreadsheet

Replace the Calculator
HACK #15

Programmers and scientists have specific calculator needs that the built-in calculator doesn't come close to meeting.

Programmers need to be able to switch bases to convert between decimal and hexadecimal. Scientists and programmers also need access to trig functions. Graphing is a nice bonus.

There are several replacement calculators available.

powerOne Scientific

The powerOne Scientific calculator (*http://www.infinitysw.com*) has the standard trig functions. It also has statistics and base conversions, as you can see in Figure 2-22.

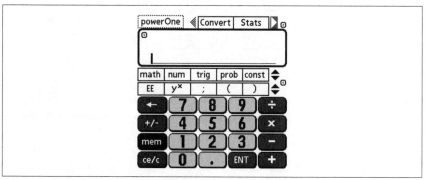

Figure 2-22. powerOne Scientific calculator

APCalc

APCalc (*http://www.palmgear.com*) is a programmable calculator. You can write your own functions and map them to buttons. This calculator comes with standard math functions (see Figure 2-23) and base conversion functions. It also has Boolean logic functions and graphing.

Figure 2-23. APCalc

EasyCalc

EasyCalc (*http://easycalc.sourceforge.net*) is an open source scientific calculator. It also supports base conversions and a reasonably large set of math and scientific functions. A small set of the functions are visible in Figure 2-24.

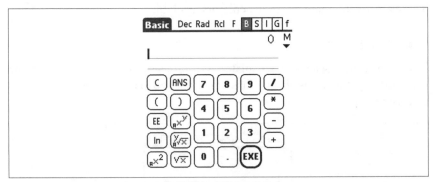

Figure 2-24. EasyCalc

Once you have found a calculator you like, you can set up the hardware buttons [Hack #44] so that the calculator soft key brings up your chosen calculator.

Turn your PDA into a Flashlight

HACK #16

When darkness falls, you can engage the backlight on your Palm and light things up.

You can turn on your Palm's backlight to act as a basic flashlight. However, you will need to disable the power-off feature if you need to use the flashlight for more than a few minutes (either that or you will have to keep turning it back on). This works nicely on a Treo with the lighted keyboard, but it also works fine on a regular Palm device. There are a couple of simple programs that do this for you.

FB Hi-Light

FB Hi-Light displays a flashlight (bright white light) and has some digital sound effects. It is available from PalmGear (*http://www.palmgear.com*; search for the name of the application there).

TealInfo/Teal Light

The program TealInfo from TealPoint Software (*http://www.tealpoint.com*) allows you to create and use simple interactive databases and mini-applications. One of those programs (called Folios) is Teal Light which gives you a variety of choices for turning your PDA into a flashlight. You can choose from a set of different colors and different patterns, as you can see in Figure 2-25.

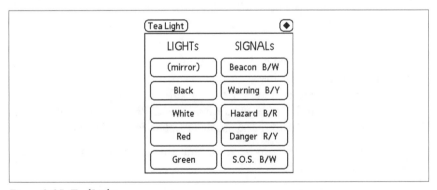

Figure 2-25. TealLight

As you can see, this is a very simple hack—the programs give you some neat options, though. Keep this idea in mind if you need a flashlight and all you have with you is your Palm device.

Hacking the Hack

You can also easily create your own flashlight program. Run the Palm OS Developer Suite **[Hack #49]**. Create a new project and select Simple as the project type from the wizard. Make the following changes to *AppMain.c*. Note that the code you should add to the wizard-generated code is shown in bold.

```
#include "AppResources.h"

// Remember the original auto-off time
static UInt16 old_time = 0;

static Err AppStart(void)
{
    // 0 means to never automatically shut off
    old_time = SysSetAutoOffTime(0);
    FrmGotoForm(MainForm);
    return errNone;
}
static void AppStop(void)
{
    // Close all the open forms.
    FrmCloseAllForms( );

    // Restore the original auto-off time
    SysSetAutoOffTime(old_time);
}
```

If you make these changes from within the Palm Developer Suite, the project will automatically be recompiled when you save the file. Fix any errors that occur in the compilation—hopefully there will be nothing more than simple typos!

Now you are ready to download the program to your Palm device. Open up Palm Desktop and press the Install button. Browse to the location of your compiled program—you are looking for the *.prc* file. If your project was named Flashlight, then the file should be somewhere like: *c:\Program Files\PalmSource\ Palm OS Developer Suite\workspace\Flashlight\Debug\Flashlight.prc*.

HotSync your Palm Device and try running the program. You should see something like Figure 2-26.

Figure 2-26. Homebrew Flashlight application

As you can see, creating a flashlight program isn't hard. The key is the SysSetAutoOffTime() function. That allows you to disable (and re-enable when you are finished) the auto shut-off feature. To get fancy looking displays, you can use the resource editor in the Palm OS Developer Suite to set a bitmap as the background for the main form. You can also remove the text or change it to something wittier.

Run Linux on Your Palm

Although it's not the Palm version of Linux that will no doubt blow our socks off when it eventually arrives, uClinux is a good way to play around with an alternative operating system on your Palm.

If you haven't heard already, Palm is switching operating systems, and in the not-so-distant future, Palm-Powered will mean Linux-Powered, but with all the elegance and grace of the current Palm OS. It's going to take a while, though. If you want to give Linux a whirl on a Palm right now, it's quick and easy. You won't get any of the graphical goodness you'll eventually get with the future version of Palm OS, but you will have a chance to play around a bit and run this powerful operating system right on your little handheld.

Unfortunately, Linux doesn't run on a lot of Palms. The good news is that it runs on a lot of older popular models, such as the IIIe, IIIx, V, Vx, and even some of the m series. You can usually find these Palms very cheaply [Hack #50], so you can play around with this on the cheap. In fact, when I bought a used Palm Vx for $30, it included a USB-to-serial adapter, which was worth nearly the price I paid for both items!

Boot Linux on Your Palm

The simplest way to get Linux running on a Palm is to pick a well-supported Palm, such as the Vx, and download a binary release of Linux from *http://palm-linux.sourceforge.net/*. At the time of this writing, they had versions that worked with the m500 as well as a bunch of older models. What you'll get is a small PRC file (such as *uClinuxPalm.prc*) that has the Linux distribution and a bootloader. Install the PRC on your Palm, and you're just about ready to launch Linux.

I say just about, because you need a couple of things. First, you need to be prepared to sacrifice everything in your Palm's storage. After you launch Linux, you'll lose all your settings, appointments, contacts, and even installed applications. You can reset your Palm and go back into the Palm OS, but it will be as if you'd performed a hard reset.

Second, you need a way to talk to the Palm. Unfortunately, if you want to interact with the Linux operating system running on your Palm, you need to use a serial connection and a terminal program. So, you won't be taking your Linux-powered Palm on the go with you. Here's what you need to do to get this all working.

Setting up the serial connection. If you've got a recent notebook computer, a Mac, or legacy-free PC, there's a good chance you don't have a classic serial port. However, there are many USB to serial adapters that can do the trick. The PalmConnect USB kit, shown in Figure 2-27, is a small dongle that will work for Windows and Linux users.

Figure 2-27. The PalmConnect USB kit

Although it ships with a CD-ROM, the PalmConnect hardware is of an old enough vintage that you should check *http://www.palm.com* to see if there are any updates to the driver (Mac OS X users will not be able to use the PalmConnect kit for this, since the Mac OS X drivers do not represent the device as a serial port). Also, Keyspan (*http://www.keyspan.com*) makes a variety of USB to Serial adapters that work with Windows, Mac OS X, and Linux.

Once you've installed the USB to serial adapter, you need to figure out where it lives. On Linux and Mac OS X, serial ports appear as files in the */dev* directory. On Windows, they appear as COM ports. Table 2-2 shows some possible candidates for serial ports for systems with both USB to serial and built-in serial ports.

Table 2-2. Possible serial port assignments

Operating system	USB to serial	Built-in
Windows	COM5 and higher	COM1 through COM4
Linux	*/dev/ttyUSB0* and higher	*/dev/ttyS0* through */dev/ttyS3*
Mac OS X	*/dev/tty.usbserial*	n/a

Installing Palm Linux. Installing Linux on your Palm is as easy as installing the PRC I mentioned earlier. On Windows or Mac OS X, set up Palm Desktop and use Quick Install to install the PRC. The next time you perform a HotSync, Palm Linux will be installed. On Linux or Unix, you can use the pilot-xfer utility to install it:

```
$ PILOTRATE=115200 pilot-xfer -p /dev/ttyS0 -i uClinuxPalm.prc


Listening to port: /dev/ttyS0

Please press the HotSync button now... Connected

Installing uClinuxPalm.prc                    Time elapsed: 0:01:26
```

Be sure to set the PILOTRATE to the maximum you feel your hardware can comfortably support. It took 1 minute, 30 seconds at 115200 bps, but 13 minutes at the default speed!

Once it's installed, you'll see a Loader icon in the launcher, as shown in Figure 2-28.

Figure 2-28. The Palm Linux loader

Booting Linux. Before you boot Linux, you should start talking to the serial port. If you're on Mac OS X or Windows, you've probably still got HotSync running and listening on the serial port. Since this will prevent you from opening a terminal session with the serial port, be sure to release the serial port before you proceed. You can either launch HotSync and configure it to not use the serial port, or shut it down altogether. If you do tell it to stop using the serial port, you'll need to switch it back before you can perform a HotSync again.

Once you've shut down HotSync, you can open a session with the serial port. On Windows, launch HyperTerminal (open the Start menu, choose Programs → Accessories → Communications → HyperTerminal) and open a session with the serial port your Palm is connected to. You should use a serial port speed of 9600, and leave the rest of the settings at their defaults. On Mac OS X or Linux, you can use the screen program to connect to the serial port, as in **screen /dev/ttyS0** (use Ctrl-A, K to end your session). You won't see anything at first, but once you make this connection, you're ready to boot Linux.

To boot Linux, tap the Palm Loader icon. You'll get the warning shown in Figure 2-29. Tap Boot Linux, and your serial port session will fill up with boot messages:

```
FFFFFFFFFFFFFFFFFFFFFFFFFFFFFFFFFFFFFFFFFFFFFFFFFFFFFFFFFFFFFFFF
FFFFFFFFFFFFFFFFFFFFFFFFFFFFFFFFFFFFFFFFFFFFFFFFFFFFFFFFFFFFFFFF
FFFFFFFFFFFFFFFFFFFFFFFFFFFFFFFFFFFFFFFFFFFRBCK
68EZ328 DragonBallEZ support (C) 1999 Rt-Control, Inc
```

```
uClinux/MC68EZ328
Flat model support (C) 1998,1999 Kenneth Albanowski, D. Jeff Dionne
PalmV support by Lineo Inc. <jeff@uClinux.com>
Console driver (without boot console): mono mc68328 40x26, 1 virtual
    console (max 63)
Calibrating delay loop..
```

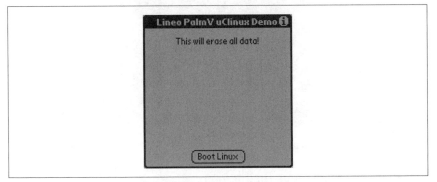

Figure 2-29. The Palm Linux warning

There will be a short delay, and then the boot messages will scroll across your screen. As this is all happening, the uClinux logo appears on the Palm, as shown in Figure 2-30. Once Linux is fully booted, your serial session will display a shell prompt:

```
Welcome to
```

```
For further information check:
http://www.uclinux.org/

Execution Finished, Exiting?
Sash command shell (version 1.1.1)
/>
```

Congratulations, you've got Linux running on your Palm. When you're ready to go back to the Palm OS, you can type **reboot** and press return, or simply do a soft reset.

Figure 2-30. Palm Linux is up and running

Roll Your Own Palm Linux Distribution

uClinux makes it possible to put together your own Linux distribution for your Palm, but it takes a bit of work to get all the pieces together. The good news is, once you've got the necessary tools, it's pretty easy to build a bootable Linux image for your Palm. In theory, you just need a cross-compiler, Palm's PRC tools, and the uClinux source. The bad news is that I could not successfully compile a kernel for my Palm Vx using the latest releases of these packages. The good news is that there is a well-documented combination of versions that works like a charm. For more information on this combination, see *http://www.ucdot.org/article.pl?sid=03/02/07/1329233*. Here's what I grabbed to get it all working:

An m68k cross-compiler

This toolchain runs on x86 Linux and compiles the kernel and userland applications into binaries that run on the Motorola CPU inside older Palms. You should grab the *m68k-elf-tools-20020410.tar.gz* file from *http://www.uclinux.org/pub/uClinux/m68k-elf-tools* and extract it into your root directory (/), which installs the cross-compiler into */usr/local*.

PRC tools

Palm's PRC tools are yet another cross-compiler, but are designed for building Palm OS applications. Since the uClinux launcher is a Palm OS executable, you need Palm's PRC tools to compile it. You can download the correct version of the PRC Tools at *http://www.uclinux.org/pub/uClinux/palm-tools/*. You should grab both *m68k-palmos-coff.tools-990108-linux-x86-glibc.tar.gz* and *prc-tools-0.5.0-5.i386.rpm*. If you're on a Linux platform that doesn't support RPM, such as Ubuntu, use the alien utility to convert the RPM into a native package and install it. Extract the *tar.gz* file into your root directory

The kernel

Once you have PRC Tools and the m68k-elf toolchain installed, you can grab the uClinux source distribution. The file *http://www.uclinux.org/pub/uClinux/dist/uClinux-dist-20020701.tar.gz* worked fine for my Palm Vx. Extract this file into a working directory, *cd* into the top-level directory (*uCLinux-dist*), and run **make xconfig** to configure everything.

Here's how I built Linux for my Palm Vx:

1. Select Target Platform Selection from the menu, choose 3com/PalmIIIx for the Vendor/Product, linux-2.0.x for the Kernel Version, and uC-libc for the Libc Version.

2. Make sure that Customize Kernel Settings is set to y and click Main Menu. Click Save and Exit. Now the kernel options appear. Under the kernel options:

    a. Enter the Platform Dependent Setup section and set the CPU to MC68EZ328, enable PalmV Support, and scroll all the way down to set "Kernel executes from" to RAM.

    b. Click Next to proceed to General Setup, enable ZFlat Support, click Main Menu to return to the main menu.

    c. Enter the Networking Options, and disable TCP/IP networking.

    d. Click Next to proceed to the Network Device Support, and click n under Network Device Support. This disables all network devices.

    e. Click Main Menu to return to the main menu and click Save and Exit.

3. You should be returned to the shell from which you ran make xconfig. Run the command make dep && make.

When it's done compiling, you should have a file called *uClinuxPalm.prc* in the *images/* subdirectory. If something goes wrong, check out *http://www.ucdot.org/article.pl?sid=03/02/07/1329233*, which goes into this process in more detail. Once you've got it compiled, you can install the PRC file as described earlier in this hack.

You might get bored with the limits of running Linux on your Palm in the way described in this hack. Fortunately, you can go a bit further with some other gadgets. uClinux is used for both Nintendo DS Linux (*http://www.dslinux.org/*) and iPod Linux (*http://www.ipodlinux.org*).

Also, there are many inexpensive embedded systems and single board computers that are capable of running uClinux. Figure 2-31 shows my Nintendo DS running uClinux with the boot messages at the top and the virtual keyboard on the bottom touchscreen.

—*Brian Jepson*

Figure 2-31. uClinux running on the Nintendo DS

## CHAPTER THREE

Play Games
Hacks 18–22

Gaming on a Palm device won't rival a console or hardcore gaming PC. On the other hand, you can't slip your console into your pocket, either (and the PlayStation Portable, for all its power, is still about twice the size of your Palm). Mobile gaming is different from home gaming, but it is still fun. The hacks in this chapter help you make the most of your mobile gaming.

If you go back 15 or 20 years and look at PCs from that era, a Palm device starts to look good. With a screen of up to 320×480 pixels and 64K colors, a Palm puts older systems to shame. Thus, emulation becomes a real possibility. Remakes look much better on the Palm than they did on the original platforms.

Modern Palm games provide interesting challenges in short bursts. Many current Palm games also add a multiplayer element to keep the games interesting.

HACK #18 Master the Dungeon

There are several programs that can help you with many chores associated with role-playing. These include dice rolling and mapping programs. But there are also adventuring kits (for players) and Dungeon Master (DM) aids.

If your idea of a pen-and-paper gaming session involves a bunch of people huddled around a table, rolling dice and consulting rule books, you'll need to add another prop to this image. Imagine that the dice spend most of their time in their velvet sack, and that the dungeon master and players put away their pens, pencils and papers in favor of a Palm and stylus. Here are some programs that will help keep the game rolling.

TS-ShadowDice

TS-ShadowDice (*http://www.freewarepalm.com/games/ts-shadowdice.shtml*) is a specialized dice roller for ShadowRun. ShadowRun has a unique approach to rolling dice. If you roll a six (on a six-sider), then you roll again and add the result. If you roll another six, you keep going. Thus, you can get numbers like 11, 13, or even 25 out of a single six-sided die. The TS-ShadowDice program knows how to re-roll sixes and add the results. In ShadowRun, you try to meet or exceed a target number which represents the difficulty of the action you are attempting. Each die that meets or exceeds the target number is called a *success*. TS-ShadowDice can tell you how many successes you have for a given number of dice against a particular target number. It can also track your character's current physical and mental conditions, which has an effect on your target numbers.

DicePro

DicePro (*http://www.rivalgamelabs.com*), shown in Figure 3-1, is a generalized dice-rolling program. It can handle various types of dice and also understands how to roll dice for several different games.

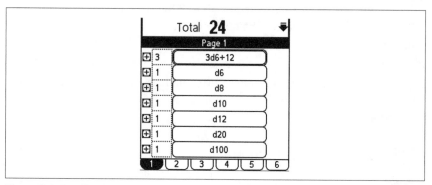

Figure 3-1. DicePro

Gamer's Die Roller

Gamer's Die Roller (*http://palm.dahm.com*) , shown in Figure 3-2 lets you set up specific combinations of dice. Need to roll four 6-siders? No problem—you can set up a button to roll that combination.

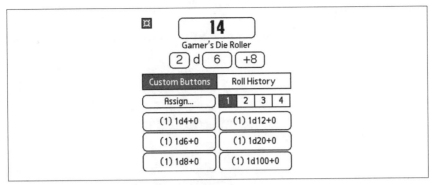

Figure 3-2. Gamer's Die Roller shown rolling 2d6+8

Cartoforge

Cartoforge (*http://www.cartoforge.com*) lets you create wilderness or dungeon maps, as seen in Figure 3-3. In addition to creating the physical layout, the application provides the ability to add text to areas on the map (such as a description of the area or the names of monsters, traps, and treasure). Cartoforge comes in a full-featured Palm version as well as a Windows desktop version.

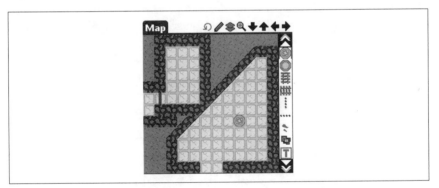

Figure 3-3. Cartoforge dungeon map

Cartoforge has its own terminology for you to learn. A campaign or adventure is divided into up to five *acts*. Each act is divided into *scenes*. A scene represents a single location. A scene contains notes and can refer to specific *cast members* (a.k.a. Non-Player Characters or NPCs or monsters). A scene also has a map. Maps can cover dungeons, wilderness, or cities. You can link characters, encounters, and treasure to locations on the map.

Dungeon Delver

Dungeon Delver (*http://www.geocities.com/iz_software/dungeondelver.html*)
provides a set of utilities for player characters. There are programs to keep
track of spells, treasure, battles fought, currently equipped items
(Figure 3-4), and more.

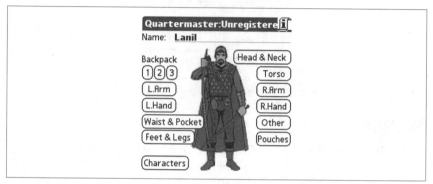

Figure 3-4. Quartermaster application, part of the Dungeon Delver suite

ShootStraight

ShootStraight (*http://www.freewarepalm.com/games/shootstraight.shtml*) helps
you compute target numbers for ShadowRun combat. An example is shown in
Figure 3-5.

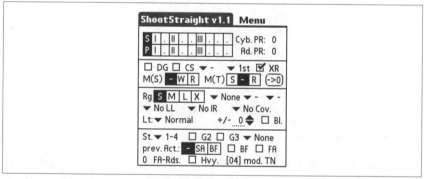

Figure 3-5. ShootStraight

MemoPad

You can even use the built-in MemoPad [Hack #5] to keep track of your characters. You can track hit points (HPs), spells, mana, actions, initiative, loot,
and equipment. You can make up your own character sheet or use
Figure 3-6 as a starting point.

```
┌─────────────────────────────────────────┐
│  Memo 1 of 1                    ┊Gaming┊ │
│  Truan's actions                          │
│                                           │
│  Magic sword                              │
│        dmg: 3D6 +17      hit: +8          │
│        parry: +14        dodge: +9        │
│  Strength bow                             │
│        dmg: 3D6 +15      hit: +10         │
│  Holy water                               │
│                                           │
│  ISP used:  10                            │
│  SDC:    7                                │
│  HP:      13                              │
│                                           │
│  Psionics:                                │
│  Bioregeneration         p. 128           │
│  Death trance            p. 128           │
│  Detect psionics         p. 127           │
│                                           │
│     ( Done ) ( Details )                  │
└─────────────────────────────────────────┘
```

Figure 3-6. MemoPad showing an example character sheet

TS-Apprentice

TS-Apprentice (*http://www.palmgear.com*), shown in Figure 3-7 tracks hit points for the party and for monsters. It can keep track of actions and initiatives, and it can roll saving throws and other dice rolls. This program is designed to be compatible with 3rd edition Dungeons and Dragons.

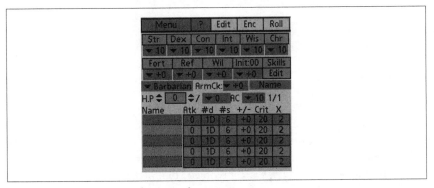

Figure 3-7. TS-Apprentice, character sheet view

As a player, you can use TS-Apprentice as a combination character sheet and dice roller. You enter in your character's vital stats (strength, dexterity, etc.) and bonuses. You also enter in your various weapons and weapon combinations. Then, TS-Apprentice can help you roll attacks, initiative, saving throws, and other dice rolls. As a DM, you can use TS-Apprentice to keep track of your important NPCs.

The Dungeon in Your Palm

With your Palm in hand, and the right assortment of tools, you're ready to master the dungeon. The following sections describe some ways you can apply these tools.

Lay out a campaign with an outliner. You can use an outliner or list manager such as ShadowPlan [Hack #11] to lay out your campaign, as seen in Figure 3-8. The top-level entries can be plot points, encounters, or significant areas (e.g., dungeons or cities). If you want to allow your players the freedom to explore the world, then you will need to be flexible about introducing these things into the campaign. You should have a range of ideas so that you can respond to whatever direction the players go.

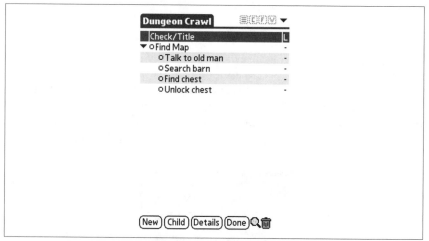

Figure 3-8. Plot points in ShadowPlan

Under each top-level item, you should go into more detail. For plot points, you might list the requirements to activate the plot point (e.g., opening the door triggers the silent alarm which summons a security team). Other plot points might be which NPCs are involved, detailed descriptions of people and places, and what the consequences of a particular plot point are. With a list manager, you can check off prerequisites and plot points as the players meet them.

For encounters, you should list the details. Describe the NPCs or monsters, any equipment they are carrying, the location, and any other details that might be important during the game. You can also write sample phrases that the NPCs might use to help you stay in character.

For locations, you want to write captivating descriptions. Unless you are using Cartoforge, you are likely to have an external map for complicated locations. For simple locations, like the inside of a tavern, you may not have a map at all. Descriptions of complicated locations may be split by rooms. In that case, you will need to key the descriptions to the map to make it easier to find the descriptions as your players progress through the map.

Simplify ShadowRun. The Game Master (GM) and players should have TS-ShadowDice and ShootStraight installed. In combat, players fill in the appropriate fields in ShootStraight—their characters' condition, range to the target, modifiers such as infrared sight, how much cover the target has, and so on. ShootStraight will then calculate the target number for that action. The GM can do the same for the NPCs. Then, the players and GM enter these target numbers into TS-ShadowDice and select the number of dice to roll. The number of dice depends on the dice pool that is being used for each action. TS-ShadowDice will then tell each player and the GM how many successes were rolled.

The next step in combat is to resist (or *stage down*) the damage. Each weapon and spell has a target number for scaling down the damage. A high-powered rifle is harder to scale down than a BB gun. So, everyone who got hit will roll either a dodge to avoid the damage or a body roll to resist the damage. Thus, each person enters the relevant target number and the number of dodge or body dice. Another roll in TS-ShadowDice will tell how much damage was avoided or reduced.

Track character changes with MemoPad. Start by creating a character sheet in MemoPad. As your character gains or loses hit points, experience, mana, or other vital statistics, you will make the corresponding changes on the character sheet. If you find a new weapon, then you can add a new weapon section listing the damage and any to-hit or other modifiers. If you go up a level, you may need to redo quite a bit of your character sheet—spells, hit points, and modifiers.

During game play, use your electronic character sheet for inspiration. It should list spells, special abilities, and important equipment. Any of these things could be useful depending on how the game goes. Having that information readily available should help spark your creativity so that you don't get stuck with nothing to do.

Map your dungeon. As a player, you can use Cartoforge to map out the dungeon as you explore. You will need to create a scene to get to the mapping tool. Give the scene a name related to the current campaign. Scroll through the mapping tiles until you find a set of dungeon hallways you like (assuming you are mapping a dungeon). Figure out a scale—each map tile representing a 10'×10' section of dungeon usually works well. Then just tap away as you go. If necessary, you can add notes to the map using the standard Cartoforge tools.

HACK #19 Discover the Best Palm Games

You don't use a Palm the same way you do a desktop computer, and games are no exception. Find out what you can expect from the gaming offerings for your Palm.

For the most part, you are unlikely to spend two straight hours playing a game on your Palm. It is more likely that you will play games in five or ten minute increments. Thus, games in which you can quickly grasp the current state of the game are good, as are games in which you can make noticeable progress in a few minutes of play.

Games like bridge or Civilization don't work well on a Palm unless you can finish an entire game in one quick session because you need to remember a large amount of information in both of those games. Tetris is a good Palm game because there is nothing to remember—the state of the game (i.e., the current pieces) is always visible. Tetris is a game that you can pick up and play for a few minutes, then set it aside and continue later.

Here are some games worth looking at, divided up into categories. This list is merely a small sample of the games available.

Role-Playing Games (RPGs)

Role-playing games put you in the role of one or more characters in a story. Typically RPGs have a fantasy theme, but there are space and detective themed RPGs as well.

Ultima. The Ultima series (1, 2, and 3) is a remake (*http://www.palmgear. com*) of the original RPGs that improves on the originals. The originals only used 16 colors for the graphics. In this remake, the graphics have been redrawn in 256 colors, as you can see in Figure 3-9.

Acedior. Acedior (*http://www.fade-team.com/content.php?content.13*) is a graphical RPG (see Figure 3-10) based on the real-life disappearance of 16 monks in the fourteenth century. The game is a fictional interpretation of this history.

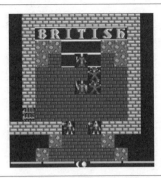

Figure 3-9. Speaking with Lord British in Ultima

Figure 3-10. Starting screen in Acedior

Strange Adventures in Infinite Space. Strange Adventures in Infinite Space (*http://www.astraware.com*) is a port to the Palm OS of a Windows game. You can play an entire game in 15 minutes, so it makes a good fit for a Palm device. The idea is to explore the stars in the randomly-generated galaxy. The items you find and aliens you meet (and occasionally destroy) form the basis of the game.

Legacy. Legacy (*http://www.redshift.hu*) is a 3D graphical RPG, as you can see in Figure 3-11. It is another original RPG designed for the Palm. You can have a party of up to four characters to explore the world. Characters can be one of a number of classes. The graphics are fairly realistic, especially given the limitations of the Palm platform.

Space Trader. In this game (*http://sourceforge.net/projects/palmtrader/*), you get to explore the galaxy as a space trader. You can also become a pirate and hunt other traders or a vigilante hunting down pirates. In any case, you will go through a variety of spaceships and accessories. No matter which path

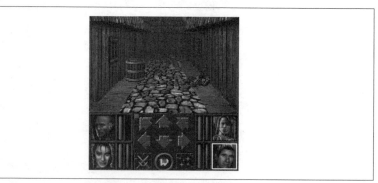

Figure 3-11. Legacy, exploring town

you choose, you will still be buying (or stealing) and selling goods. You can see an example from the game in Figure 3-12.

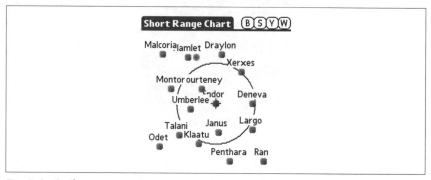

Figure 3-12. Short-range map in Space Trader

Kyle's Quest. Kyle's Quest (*http://www.crimsonfire.com/kq2/*) is a typical third-person RPG, as you can see in Figure 3-13. It comes with a map editor which has enabled other people to create maps (many are available for download from the Kyle's Quest web site). It is very popular, so there are plenty of add-on maps for it.

Strategy

There is no shortage of strategy games for the Palm. Whether you're playing a classic board game or a more complicated title, these are a great way to get your game on.

Chess (various). Chess (see Figure 3-14) works because you can play an entire game in a few minutes, but you can play a longer game if you have the time. There are a number of different chess games available and even some chess variants. Try several of them to see if any fit you.

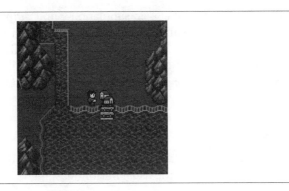

Figure 3-13. Kyle's Quest

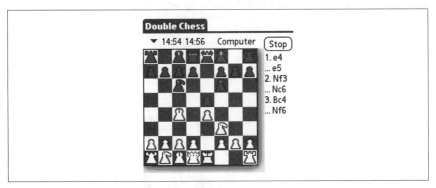

Figure 3-14. Sample chess game

Strategic Commander. Strategic Commander (*http://www.zindaware.com*) is a resource gathering, spaceship building, and galaxy conquering game (see Figure 3-15). You try to balance between producing ships, building factories and research labs, colonizing new planets, and fighting enemy ships and taking over enemy planets. It is turn-based, so you can make some moves and come back to the game later.

Figure 3-15. Strategic Commander, map view

SimCity. SimCity is the classic simulation game (*http://www.ateliersoftware. com/palm/scc.html*). This version doesn't work with Palm OS 5, but if you have an earlier machine it works fine. This is the official port of the desktop game. There is also an open-source version called PocketCity (*http:// pocketcity.sourceforge.net/*) which works with Palm OS 5, but it is still in an early stage.

Puzzle Games

Puzzle games are quick and easy to get into, and the stylus makes for an interesting escape from the usual button-mashing you find on other systems.

Tetris. Tetris (*http://www.handmark.com*) is probably the best-known puzzle game. In Tetris, the object is to drop various shaped blocks to fill up a row. Every time you fill a row, that row is cleared. You have to avoid having a block get stuck at the top, on top of other blocks. Tetris is a great game for a Palm device because you can always see where you are with the game, as you can see in Figure 3-16.

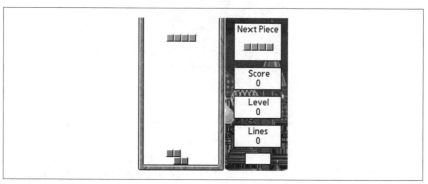

Figure 3-16. Tetris

Bejeweled. Bejeweled (*http://www.astraware.com*) is a Palm OS original. It is as addictive as Tetris without having quite the same twitch component. Bejeweled has a bit more thinking and strategy than Tetris.

Vexed. Vexed (Figure 3-17) is an open-source puzzle game (*http://vexed. sourceforge.net*). In this game, you try to eliminate blocks by moving them next to a matching block. There are multiple levels with different challenges.

You can also play classic games [Hack #21] with emulators or remakes. Other entertainment choices include watching videos [Hack #28] and listening to music [Hack #25].

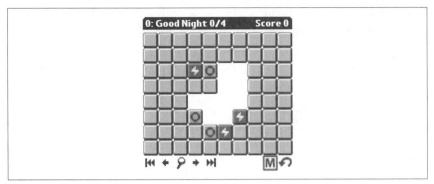

Figure 3-17. Starting level in Vexed

Play Multiplayer Games

HACK #20

Looking for more of a challenge in your mobile gaming? Try playing against another person for that extra edge.

Multiplayer Palm games provide several different ways to connect with opponents. The basic connection methods are infrared (IR), direct Bluetooth connection, and using the Internet. Multiplayer games may only support one or two of these methods—a few support all three.

Infrared

For an infrared connection, you can only connect to one person at a time. You need to be fairly close together, depending on the strength of the IR transmitters in both Palm devices. Pacific Neo-Tek, the maker of OmniRemote, has some notes on effective transmitting ranges for various devices (*http://www.pacificneotek.com/range.htm*).

You need to keep the devices pointed at each other while you play. To test the IR connection, first try beaming a memo back and forth. Test both ways to check the range on each of the transmitters. If the range isn't sufficient, then you can look at getting a more powerful add-on IR transmitter **[Hack #41]**.

Starting an infrared game is straightforward. Both players start the game on their Palm devices. One player initiates an IR game (details vary depending on the game). The other player then connects to the IR game.

Direct Bluetooth Connection

If you are using Bluetooth to connect to the Internet, then that is treated as Internet gaming. A game using a direct Bluetooth connection allows two or more people (depending on the game) to play together. For a direct

Bluetooth game, all of the players must be within Bluetooth range. So you can use Bluetooth to play across the room but not across the country.

If you want to use a direct Bluetooth connection, but you are using Bluetooth for Internet access [Hack #34], then you may need to disable your Internet access while you are gaming.

All of the players should start the game, and then one person initiates a session. The other players join that player's game.

Internet

If you are connected to the Internet [Hack #34], and the game you are playing supports it, then you can use the Internet to play with other people. Some games have specific servers that you have to connect to. Other games let you run servers on your own desktop machine. Either way, you will most likely need the IP address of a server for Internet gaming. Some games may be able to locate servers on their own.

If you have a choice of multiplayer connection types, what should you choose? For a local gaming group, you can use IR or Bluetooth. Otherwise (or if you want to try your skills on a wider audience), you can use an Internet connection.

Multiplayer Games

There are various types of games which support multiple players. Implementations of traditional board and card games, such as chess and poker, sometimes have multiplayer modes. Shooting games and real-time strategy games also occasionally support multiplayer mode.

Following are some games that support multiple players. You can find more multiplayer games by going to a Palm directory site and searching for multiplayer, Bluetooth, infrared, or Internet.

RifleSLUGs-W (http://www.palm-games.penreader.com/rifleslugs-II/)
> RifleSLUGs (see Figure 3-18) is a strategy game for one or two players. You play an army of slugs that is trying to defeat the other army. RifleSLUGs supports multiple players through IR, Bluetooth, or an Internet connection.

ChessGenius (http://www.chessgenius.com)
> ChessGenius (Figure 3-19) supports infrared play against another person who is armed with their own copy of ChessGenius.

Figure 3-18. RifleSLUGs startup screen

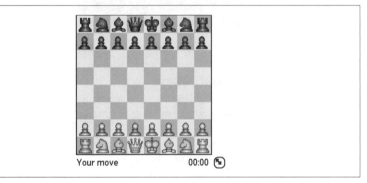

Figure 3-19. ChessGenius

Multiplayer Championship Poker—Texas Hold'em (http://www.realdice.com)
 Multiplayer Championship Poker—Texas Hold'em supports multiple
 players through both IR and Bluetooth. You can see a human player versus multiple computer players in Figure 3-20.

There are many other games that have multiplayer support. You can also
play web-based games with a browser [Hack #37]. For example, play Blackjack
(*http://blackjack.fon.ungames.com/index.php*) with nothing more than a standard web browser—no extra plug-ins are required. Note that Flash is not
supported by most Palm browsers (although some devices, such as some
Clié models, do support Flash), so you will not be able to play Flash-based
web games.

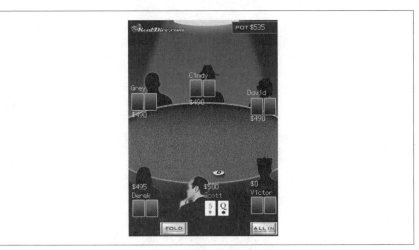

Figure 3-20. Playing Multiplayer Championship Poker – Texas Hold'em

 Play Classic Games

#21   Do you want to relive the early days of computer games? It's easy to find emulators that let you play the real thing, or remakes that kick the originals up a notch.

Any Palm can play classic games, but if you are really into playing games you should look at Tapwave's Zodiac (*http://www.tapwave.com*). The Zodiac has familiar game controls and is laid out in landscape mode (480× 320 pixels) to work better with games. The Zodiac also has a graphics accelerator and a stereo headphone jack. It comes in two flavors—a 32 MB model for $270 and a 128 MB model for $350.

   As of this writing, Tapwave had announced that they were ceasing production of the Zodiac, which is unfortunate, because it is an excellent gaming system. As stores clear their inventories, you may be able to find deals on these hand-helds. However, as people realize the potential with these Zodiacs, the prices may go up to keep with demand. So look carefully and compare prices.

Note that emulators tend to be more faithful to the original games while remakes tend to look and play better on Palm devices, unless your playing style depends on specific timing (or bugs) in the original games. For example, if you use patterns to complete Pac-Man mazes, they are more likely to work on an emulator than on a remake.

Emulators

There are several good emulators available for Palm OS.

Once you have an emulator, you need to find legal games for it. You can get legal games by searching the Web for games that have been legally released (such as new open-source or homebrew games). Sites such as *http://www.pdroms.de* have legal free ROMs, usually in the public domain, and often of a high quality. You can buy original games (e.g., purchase arcade cabinets or circuit boards off of eBay) and use an EEPROM reader/burner to extract the ROM image. Download the image to your PDA to start playing. Or you can purchase ROMs legally from StarROMs (*http://www.starroms.com*).

CaSTaway (http://www.codejedi.com). CaSTaway (Figure 3-21) is an Atari ST emulator. You will need to get an image of the operating system (TOS) and a disk or ROM image of the games you want to run.

```
CaSTaway/Palm
Path:/Palm/Programs/AtariST/
Drive A:
Drive B:



    Go        □ FPS?   ☑ Sound On?
```

Figure 3-21. CaSTaway, Atari ST emulator

Kalemsoft (http://www.kalemsoft.com). Kalemsoft sells emulators for the Nintendo Entertainment System (NES), Sega Game Gear / Master System, and PC Engine / Turbo Grafx-16. The NES emulator is shown in Figure 3-22.

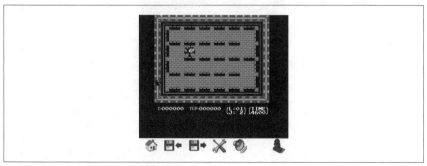

Figure 3-22. NesEm, a Nintendo emulator running Bomb Sweeper

vPCB Arcade Emulator(http://www.freewarepalm.com/games/vpcbarcadeemu-latorforpalmos.shtml). vPCB Arcade Emulator is an open source emulator for arcade games.

xCade (http://www.codejedi.com). xCade is a commercial arcade emulator. Both vPCB and xCade support different games, so look at both of them if you are interested in a specific game.

Liberty (http://www.gambitstudios.com). Liberty is a commercial emulator for the Nintendo GameBoy. You can see a sample game in Figure 3-23.

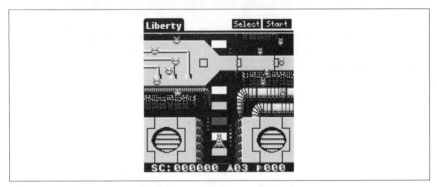

Figure 3-23. Liberty GameBoy emulator running Alien Planet

Little John PalmOS (http://yoyofr.fr.st/). The Little John emulator is an open-source emulator for multiple systems. You can see the startup screen for the SNES system in Figure 3-24.

Figure 3-24. Little John multi-system emulator

PalmMame. PalmMame (*http://www.pocketdimension.com/PalmMAME.html*) is a multi-arcade machine emulator that can play ROMs from arcade machines.

There are more emulators available that are specific to the Zodiac (*http://zodiacgamer.emuboards.com/modules.php?name=News&new_topic=6*). If you are really serious about emulators, you might find something to spark your interest.

Remakes

There are some high-quality remakes of popular games from the 1980s and 1990s. These games have been rewritten to run natively on Palm devices without needing any emulators. In some cases, the remakes have actually improved on the originals.

Ultima series (http://www.palmgear.com). Ultima (see Figure 3-25) is a traditional computer role-playing game. Several titles in the Ultima series (Ultima 1, 2, and 3) have been redone as native Palm applications. The ports actually improve on the originals. All of the graphics have been redrawn in 256 colors instead of the original 16. The playability is very good—this series seems to work well on Palm devices.

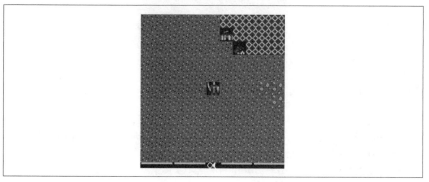

Figure 3-25. Ultima series

Archon (http://www.emperor-studios.de/). Archon (see Figure 3-26) is a fantasy strategy game, loosely related to chess. It combines a touch of strategy with action. When one piece moves onto another, the play switches to a battleground where the two pieces fight for control of the square. The loser is removed from the board.

Figure 3-26. Archon title screen

Atari Retro (http://www.gomdm.com/pda_palmos_games.asp). The Atari Retro package contains seven classic games: Asteriods, Breakout, Centipede (see Figure 3-27), Missile Command, Pong, Adventure, and Yar's Revenge.

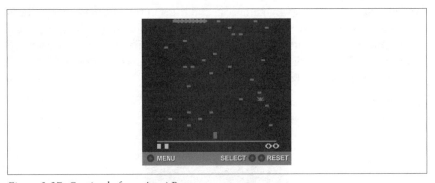

Figure 3-27. Centipede from Atari Retro

Of course there are many more games and emulators available than are listed here. If you are interested in classic gaming, you will find information on the Web. You can also find more information in the book *Gaming Hacks* (O'Reilly, 2005) and *Retro Gaming Hacks* (O'Reilly, 2005).

HACK #22   Boost Your Online Gaming

A Palm device can be a useful tool when playing online games on your desktop machine.

Your Palm device can store information for use in online games. You can also use a Palm device to look up information on the Web without disturbing your game.

Storing Information in MemoPad

You can store all sorts of useful information in MemoPad for online gaming, as you can see in Figure 3-28. You can store spell lists and locations of quest items. You can store descriptions of skills. You can record which loot items are useful in trade skills and which are junk. You can track the skill levels of your characters in tradeskills. You can also use MemoPad to hold future specs for your character—do you go heavy in bow or heavy in melee?

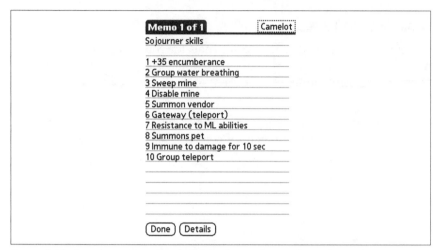

Figure 3-28. *Sojourner Master Level abilities for Dark Age of Camelot*

Track Quests with the To Do List

Use the To Do List to track quests, if the online game doesn't have a good quest manager. You can create a category for each multi-step quest or use priorities to track substeps of quests within a single category. This can be very useful if a quest has a number of subquests that can be completed in any order.

Look Up Information on the Web

If your Palm device is connected to the Internet [Hack #34], then you can surf the Web [Hack #37] to find information on your game. Most games have a few top quality sites that provide maps, quest info, bestiaries, and more. Sometimes it is easier to snag info using a separate machine or Palm device than it is to tab out of the game. You can sometimes find text-based walkthroughs or strategy guides that you can download to your Palm device.

PDAPortal (*http://www.pdaportal.com*) is a directory of PDA-friendly web sites which includes some game sites.

Calculator

Use the calculator for figuring prices for tradeskill items or other game-related computations. In the standard calculator, you can recall earlier calculations which can be useful if you end up doing the same thing over and over. If you have replaced the standard calculator [Hack #15], then you can program in useful formulas like how much mana you will get for an increase in *Intelligence* or how many hit points an increase in *Stamina* will give you.

Game-Specific Tools

Sometimes you can find game-specific tools for your online game. For Everquest, there was a mana calculator that would take the relevant stats (primary casting attribute, level, and class) and tell you how much mana you had.

The World of Warcraft site (*http://www.worldofwarcraft.com*) recommends using a PDA to keep track of items if you are going to be buying or selling a lot.

Multimedia
Hacks 23–28

It's time to load up the old multimedia utility belt. Portable DVD player. Check. iPod. Check. Voice recorder. Electronic book reader.

That utility belt fills up fast when you try to carry all your electronics. Even if you have an eVest (*http://www.scottevest.com/*), that's still a lot of stuff to carry. Plus you need spare batteries or rechargers for all of those devices.

What if you could use your Palm device to replace all those others? Granted, a Palm device won't be as efficient a music player as an iPod, and the screen isn't as big as a portable DVD player. But a Palm device can do an adequate job of replacing all of those devices, and a Palm device has its own unique functions as well. You can play games and use the standard applications on a Palm device—that's much harder to do on other types of electronic devices.

The following hacks explore the multimedia possibilities of Palm devices— what you need to get started, and where to obtain books, audio, video, and more.

HACK **#23**

Read Books and Articles

On most Palm devices, MemoPad is limited to notes that are 4K or less. That is fine for writing short notes to yourself, but you wouldn't want to read a large document in 4K chunks—instead, you need another solution.

There are a number of document readers available for Palm OS that allow you to read large documents. Most of the document readers use a special format called *DOC*, which should not be confused with the Microsoft Word *.doc* format. Many document readers also read their own proprietary formats that allow for font changes and other special features. Document readers typically come with converters that understand common desktop file formats.

Document Readers

The following list contains some representative document readers. This list is by no means complete. If you need additional capabilities, then you may want to search beyond the readers in this list. MemoWare (*http://www.memoware.com/mw.cgi/?screen=help_format*) has a good list of document readers. MemoWare lists the formats that document readers can understand and also has links to the actual readers themselves.

Picsel File Viewer (included on some Palm devices). Picsel File Viewer has an innovative user interface, as you can see in Figure 4-1. The interface represents documents graphically. You can zoom in or out and move through a document easily using the pen. Picsel File Viewer supports Palm DOC documents, Microsoft Word *.doc* documents, Microsoft PowerPoint documents, and HTML documents. It does require a memory card to access documents, however.

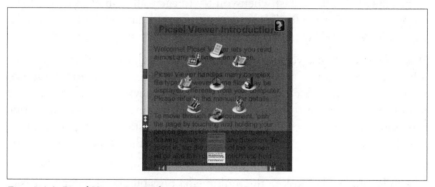

Figure 4-1. Picsel Viewer's interface

TealDoc (http://www.tealpoint.com). TealDoc provides the features you should expect in a document reader: anti-aliased fonts, full-screen mode, bookmarks, and smooth scrolling. TealDoc also lets you edit documents. You can see a sample document in Figure 4-2.

iSilo (http://www.isilo.com). iSilo supports its own compressed document format in addition to the Palm DOC format. iSilo claims that their compressed format is about 20% smaller than a Palm DOC file. The iSilo format also supports embedded images, text formatting, and hyperlinks. You can see this in action in Figure 4-3.

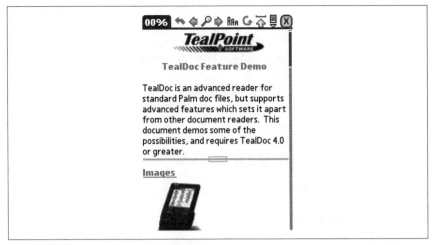

Figure 4-2. TealDoc showing a sample document

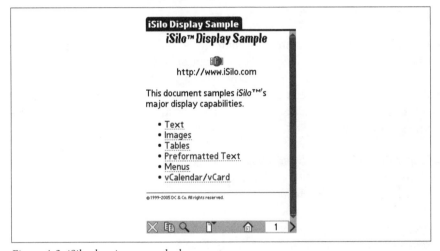

Figure 4-3. iSilo showing a sample document

CSpotRun (http://www.32768.com/bill/palmos/cspotrun/). CSpotRun is a free document reader. You can switch between landscape and portrait mode or switch to full screen mode. CSpotRun supports bookmarks and selecting different fonts. You can see the interface in Figure 4-4.

Weasel Reader (http://www.gutenpalm.sourceforge.net). Weasel Reader is an open-source document reader. It supports the standard Palm DOC format and compressed text files using the same compression algorithms as gzip. It supports high-resolution devices and also provides full annotation support, including links to where the annotation occurs.

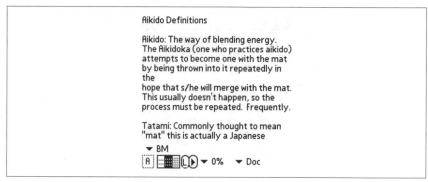

Figure 4-4. CSpotRun displaying text

Finding Documents to Read

Some document readers can understand (or convert) web pages. Those programs let you read anything on the Web. There are also some specific repositories of electronic texts on the Web.

MemoWare (http://www.memoware.com). MemoWare contains electronic documents specifically formatted for Palm document readers. Many of the texts are public domain, although there are also some texts available for purchase. Most of the documents are in the standard Palm DOC format, but some of them are formatted for particular document readers. All of the documents are clearly marked as to which format they are in.

Project Gutenberg (http://www.gutenberg.org). Project Gutenberg produces free electronic versions of books that have fallen into the public domain or that have been released by their authors into the public domain. These books are in a plain text format. You will need to search to find interesting books—Project Gutenberg has converted more than 15,000 books. PyGE (*http://pyge. sourceforge.net*) is an open source browser for Project Gutenberg.

Baen Free Library (http://www.baen.com/library/). Baen Books has put a number of their books online for free download. These books have been selected by the authors themselves—participation is entirely voluntary. Mostly the books seem to be fantasy and science fiction and are available in a number of formats.

Creating Your Own Documents

There are several programs available for converting from text, HTML, or other formats to Palm DOC formats. Many of the document readers which have their own internal formats also have converters that run on the desktop to convert various types of documents into their own formats. MemoWare has good listings of both document readers and document creators.

One good Windows program is DocReader (*http://mpickering.homeip.net/phpwiki/index.php/DocReader*). It is free software that runs under Windows, and can convert text files to and from DOC files. You can see an example of it in Figure 4-5.

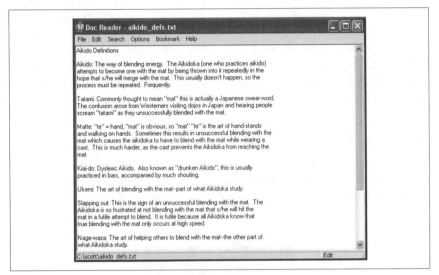

Figure 4-5. Screenshot of DocReader

With DocReader (or a similar program), you can create documents on your desktop and export them to your Palm device. You can also download text from other places and convert it into documents to read as you travel. If you write your own documents, then you can export them to a web site like MemoWare to make them available to other Palm users.

The program txt2pdbdoc (*http://homepage.mac.com/pauljlucas/software/txt2pdbdoc/*) is a command-line tool available for Unix-based systems. It is open source.

PorDiBle (*http://pordible.victoly.com/*) is a Mac OS X program which converts between DOC *pdb* files and text files. It is graphical—you can drag a text file or DOC file onto the program to convert the file. Palm Doc Converter (*http://lokisw.com/index.php?item=PalmDocConverter*) is another freeware text to DOC converter for OS X.

Improve Text Entry

#24

Everyone has their own techniques for entering text, but some simple techniques can make you more effective.

You have two main choices for handwritten text: Graffiti and Decuma. Depending on which device you have, you may have a choice between Graffiti, Graffiti 2, and Decuma. You can create *shortcuts*. A shortcut is an abbreviation that is automatically expanded for you. To create a shortcut, run the Prefs application **[Hack #46]** and select the Personal → ShortCuts category. To use a Graffiti shortcut, write the shortcut character (see Figure 4-6), followed by the abbreviation. Your PDA will automatically replace the abbreviation with the corresponding text. For devices that come with a built-in keyboard, there is no Graffiti input area. To enter the shortcut character on these devices, you need to do the following:

1. Enter the letter **s** into the text field.

2. Press the Alt key to bring up the alternate-character list.

3. Select the "shortcut" symbol at the bottom of the list. The easiest way to do this is to keep holding the Alt key for one second. Other ways are to press the Alt key three more times or to press down on the 5-way three times.

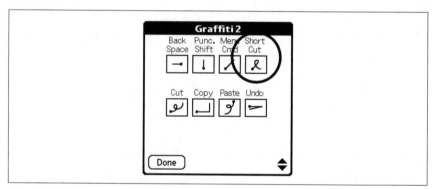

Figure 4-6. Shortcut character

If you want to be able to use Graffiti on devices with built-in keyboards (and no Graffiti area), then you can use a program called GraffitiAnywhere (*http://www. palmgear.com/index.cfm?fuseaction=software.showsoftware&prodid=45227*). This program allows you to write Graffiti strokes directly on the screen.

Another option for Graffiti 2 is to tweak the form of several hard-to-write characters. Run the Prefs application and select the Graffiti 2 category. You will see a set of buttons for the various characters which can be tuned. Tap

Graffiti Versus Graffiti 2

From a practical point of view, there are a couple of differences between Graffiti and Graffiti 2. In Graffiti, all of the letters could be formed from a single pen stroke. (To write an X, you could write the symbol for K backwards.) While this was quick (and easy for Palm devices to recognize), it also meant that you had to learn a new alphabet to begin using a Palm device.

Graffiti 2 looks much more like normal block printing. This means that many letters are formed from two strokes instead of one. The advantage is that there is less of a learning curve (unless you have learned Graffiti; then you have to switch back, and the switch can take a little while to get used to). The biggest disadvantage is that it is a bit slower to write Graffiti 2 letters than in the original Graffiti.

on a character to see the alternate form that can be used (see Figure 4-7 for an example). There may also be information about related characters. If the alternate form looks like it will be easier for you to use, check the box and press the Done button.

Figure 4-7. Graffiti 2 tuner, showing the letter t

You may also be able to set your Palm device to let you write Graffiti on the main screen instead of on the Graffiti area under the screen. Go to the Prefs application and see if you have a top-level Writing Area category. If so, select it and you will be able to switch between writing Graffiti in the silk-screened area and writing it on the main screen. If you choose to write on the main screen, then you can also choose whether or not to leave the pen strokes on the screen. This can be helpful in figuring out why your characters aren't being recognized.

Another useful item that is often overlooked appears on the Edit menu whenever you can enter text. The last item on that menu is Graffiti Help (or

Graffiti 2 Help). You can select this menu item to see a graphical view of how to draw each character. This can help if you are having problems with the recognition of a particular character. You can also draw a vertical line from the bottom of the digitizer to the top of the screen to invoke Graffiti help.

Decuma Options

Decuma (see Figure 4-8) is a continuous handwriting recognition engine. You can write multiple characters on the screen and edit them using gestures. Decuma is available standard on some devices, such as the Sony Clié. You can also find versions of Decuma (if your device didn't come with it) at *http://www.zicorp.com*. If Decuma is available as a standard part of your device, then it may replace the soft keyboard. Thus, pressing the A in the silk-screened area brings up the alphabetic tab and pressing 1 brings up the numeric tab.

Figure 4-8. Entering text with Decuma

To configure Decuma, just run the Decuma application from the launcher. The Shortcuts category lets you associate a series of stylus strokes with particular text. For example, you can set a cursive me to be your name. Setting up shortcuts for words or phrases you use a lot can save time.

The Settings tab lets you enable character recognition for characters from other languages. You can enable French, Italian, Swedish, German, and Spanish. You can also set the recognition timeout by pressing the Advanced button. The Personalize category allows you to tune the recognizer by writing your own versions of characters.

Virtual Keyboards

Most Palm devices have a virtual keyboard built-in, as you can see in Figure 4-9. Actually, they have three: an alphabetic keyboard using the QWERTY layout, an international keyboard with accented characters, and a numeric keyboard which includes symbols. You can open the alphabetic keyboard by tapping the *a* or *abc* (depending on which device you have) in the silk-screened area. You can open the numeric keyboard by tapping the *1* or *123* in the silk-screened area, as you can see in Figure 4-10. You can get to the international keyboard by opening either of the other keyboards and selecting the *Int'l* button. You can switch to the alphabetic keyboard by tapping the *abc* button, and you can reach the numeric keyboard by tapping the *123* button with any of the keyboards open.

Figure 4-9. Virtual keyboard, showing alphabetic layout

Figure 4-10. Silk-screened keyboard buttons

A third-party keyboard is available that has been designed to optimize the speed of entering text by tapping with a stylus. This keyboard is called Fitaly (*http://www.fitaly.com*). The Fitaly keyboard uses a non-QWERTY layout that's optimized to speed up single-tap text entering. The keyboard comes in two varieties: a virtual keyboard that replaces the built-in keyboard and a physical overlay for the silk-screened area.

Physical Keyboards

You can also buy full-sized folding keyboards for Palm devices [Hack #52]. These keyboards fold into approximately the same size as a PDA. The keys are nearly full size, the same as you find on a laptop. Keyboards allow you to enter text at your full typing speed. The main drawback is that you need a stable surface to put the keyboard on, since the keyboards have a tendency to fold up if you try to use them on your lap.

For devices with built-in keyboards, you can type accented characters. Press the key corresponding to the accented character you want to enter, and then press the Alt button. This will bring up a list of the different accented characters corresponding to the key you pressed. You can use the up and down arrow buttons to scroll through the list. When you have the character you want to enter selected, press the Center button to accept it, or you can just continue typing characters and it will be automatically accepted.

HACK #25 Listen to Music

Turn your Palm into a portable music player.

The first step in listening to music is to find some music to listen to. The major music players for Palm devices (AeroPlayer and Pocket Tunes) both play MP3s and Ogg Vorbis (*.ogg*) files. Ogg Vorbis is a nice format because it isn't patent-encumbered.

If a music format is patent-encumbered, that means that it might infringe on someone else's patented invention, which usually means that the number of players is limited. To write a player for a patent-encumbered format, the author needs to either take on a certain legal risk or spend the money to license the patent. You are more likely to be able to find players for formats that aren't patent-encumbered, and the players are likely to be less expensive.

There are various sources for music:

MagnaTune

MagnaTune (*http://www.magnatune.com*) is an independent Internet music label. Their tag line is "We're a record label, but we're not evil." They have previews of all of their music available for you to listen to. If you hear something you like, you can purchase and download it. Once you buy music there, you can download it as many times as you need to and in any format that you want. You can also burn a CD from the music you download.

Game sites

Many game publishers (e.g., Blizzard, *http://www.blizzard.com*) end up putting some or all of the music for their games up for free download. For example, there is music available from World of Warcraft (*http://www.worldofwarcraft.com*) If you like this type of music, you can get it legally and for free.

Creative Commons

The Creative Commons (*http://creativecommons.org/*) is a framework for specifying protections and freedoms for creative works (e.g., music, books, articles, etc.). If you search for Creative Commons on the Web and put in appropriate terms (e.g., music, jazz), then you can sometimes find music to download. You will need to check each piece of music individually to see what you are allowed to do with it.

RIAA Radar

Ever wonder how much of the money you paid for the music goes to the artist? Independent artists tend to get a higher percentage of the money than artists that work for RIAA labels. With the RIAA Radar (*http://www.magnetbox.com/riaa/*) you can check to see if the album or artist you are interested in is independent or not. You can search for independent artists who play similar music to what is on the RIAA labels.

Copy Music from Your PC to Your Palm

In addition to actually having some music to download to your Palm, you need a few more things.

If you want to listen to more than a few songs, then you need to have a memory card for your Palm device. For a Sony Clié, that means you need a Memory Stick or Memory Stick Pro. For a Palm-branded device, you need an SD or MMC card. Pick a card that will hold as much music as you want to carry with you, plus has enough space for anything else (like videos) that you might want. A typical song (four minutes long) requires 3.84 MB, so if you get a 512 MB memory card, you can store up to 133 songs. Note that the size of a song depends primarily on two things: the quality it was recorded at (e.g., a song recorded at 44 kHz requires twice as much memory as one recorded at 22 kHz) and the length of the song. Thus, if you have a choice of quality on songs, you can get more songs by picking songs at a lower quality.

If you have a flash memory card reader that you can plug into your PC, now's the time to use it. There are few things slower than copying large files to your Palm over HotSync. Because these readers are inexpensive (typically under $30), they are well worth the money for the convenience they give you. When you plug the memory card into the card reader, and the card reader into your PC, the card will appear as a hard drive attached to your computer. Copy the files to the */Audio* folder on the card, and then safely eject the card reader from your computer; on a Windows PC, right-click on the *Safely Remove Hardware* icon in the system tray (on the lower right of your screen) and select *Safely remove USB Mass Storage Device*. On a Mac, drag the drive to the Trash to eject it.

About Flash Memory

Flash memory is the general term for device-specific terms like Memory Stick, Compact Flash, and SD. Flash memory is a form of EEPROM (Electrically Erasable Programmable Read-Only Memory). Technically, this means a couple of things. Flash memory is a bit slower to write than regular RAM. However, it has the advantage that the memory doesn't go away when the power is removed. That's why flash memory cards don't have batteries. And that's also why you can remove a memory card and not lose any data on it (assuming you don't damage the card while carrying it around, of course). You only need power for flash memory when reading or writing it.

Because flash is a specialized form of memory, its costs are closer to RAM than to hard disks. Thus, you will see a 1 or 2 GB memory card (of any brand) priced at about half of a 20 GB iPod. The prices for Flash memory will continue to come down as chips keep getting cheaper.

If you want to use HotSync to copy the files, the next step depends on which type of device you have.

Sony Clié. The next thing you need to do is install software on your PC to support transferring songs to the card on your Clié. This program is called "Data Export" and is only available on Windows machines. If you didn't install it when you initially installed the Palm Desktop software, then you will need to install it now off of the original CD.

Your PDA should already have the "Data Import" application installed. If not, then you will need to install it from the original CD as well.

The next step is to use the Data Export (PC side) and Data Import (PDA side) programs to transfer your music to the memory card in your PDA.

Palm-branded device. To transfer music (or other files) to an SD card on a Palm-branded device, use the *Quick Install* program on the desktop. Then just do a normal HotSync to transfer the files.

Listening to Music

Your device may have a built-in player (such as Real Player) that you can use to listen to the music that you copied over. If your Palm device did not include a music player, then you can download either AeroPlayer (*http:// www.aerodrome.us/*), as seen in Figure 4-11 or Pocket Tunes (*http://www. pocket-tunes.com/*) as seen in Figure 4-12. There is also MMPlayer (*http:// www.mmplayer.com*), which can play movies as well as music (see Figure 4-13). MMPlayer can also play music and videos from internal memory in addition to playing from a memory card. If you are only going to use internal memory, though, you will be limited in how much music you can store. But if you only want to store a couple of songs, then you can save yourself the expense of a memory card. The Kinoma Player (*http://www. kinoma.com*) also plays music and videos and can play music and video out of internal memory. Try the demo versions of these programs and see which you prefer.

Figure 4-11. AeroPlayer

The programs will automatically detect and load the music files from the memory card or internal memory and will give you a default playlist with all of the songs listed. You can also create separate playlists that cover a subset of the songs—for example, "morning wake-up songs" and "evening unwind songs."

Figure 4-12. Pocket Tunes

Figure 4-13. MMPlayer

You can listen to songs with the built-in speaker if you have to, but you are better off using a set of headphones. The quality will be much better and you will be less likely to annoy people around you (well, at least by playing music—if you're annoying in other ways, the headphones won't help). Look for headphones with a volume control—that will make it easier to adjust the volume without having to fumble around with your PDA. See *http://www. headphone.com* for lots of details on headphones.

Once you have your playlist set and are actually listening to music, then you get to uncover the secret of the "Hold" button that many Palm devices have. This is usually an alternate position of the power slider on the Palm device. What this does is shut off the screen while leaving the Palm running so you can listen to music without killing your battery. Note, however, that a Palm device is probably not going to beat a dedicated digital music player for battery life, even with the screen off. Tapwave Zodiac users can put the device into Hold while playing music by pressing the menu button and selecting Hold from the Options menu. The Zodiac will also switch into Hold automatically when the automatic shut-off timer is reached. The Zodiac seems to run a custom music player. If it works for you, great. If not, try one of the alternatives to see if it meets your needs.

HACK #26 Record Voice Memos

Sometimes it is faster and easier to speak a memo than it is to write one.

Some Palm devices come equipped to record voice memos. Devices such as the Tungsten C, Tungsten T, Tungsten T3, and Zire 72 come with the Voice Memo application. Even on these devices, however, you will need to purchase a hands-free headset from palmOne to record voice memos. The headset has a button for recording memos. Push the button to start recording, push it again to stop. Or you can start and stop recording from the Voice Memo application itself.

People seem to have better luck accessing voice memos on their Palm device if the memos are stored on a memory card rather than in internal memory.

Voice Memo syncs with the desktop. On Windows, there is a plug-in for the desktop that allows you to manage and listen to voice memos.

Software Solutions

For Tungsten, Treo, and some Zire models, you have another choice. You can buy software that makes use of a headset to record voice memos. These programs provide the same sorts of functions as the built-in Voice Memo application, except they work on a wider range of devices.

Personal Audio Recorder PRO. Personal Audio Recorder PRO (*http://www. toysoft.ca*, see Figure 4-14) provides many useful features, including one button recording, playback of memos on the Palm device (including a pause function), and importing and exporting of memos from and to a memory card. Once you have voice memos on a memory card, you can use a memory card reader on your PC to transfer the voice memos. Also, Personal Audio Recorder PRO allows you to email voice memos and set voice memos as alarms.

Palm Dictate. Palm Dictate (*http://www.nch.com.au/palmdictate/*, Figure 4-15) isn't designed for voice memos in particular. Instead, it is designed for people who need to do dictation and have it typed up. Palm Dictate allows you to dictate into your Palm device, and then it automatically emails the audio out to be transcribed. There are also versions of Palm Dictate available that encrypt the emails to comply with legal regulations.

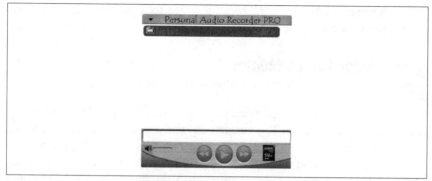

Figure 4-14. Personal Audio Recorder PRO

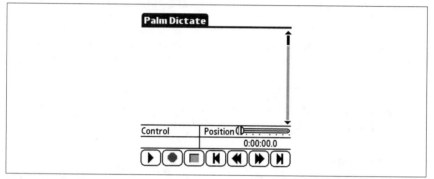

Figure 4-15. Palm Dictate

mVoice. mVoice (*http://www.motionapps.com*) is a voice memo recorder for Treos. It comes with the standard features: storing voice memos in internal memory or on a memory card, playing memos, appending to existing memos, and moving memos between internal memory and a memory card. You can transfer voice messages from one Palm device to another by email or by beaming them via infrared.

SoundRec. SoundRec (*http://www.infinityball.com*) is a free voice memo recorder. It works on any Palm OS 5 device that has sound recording capabilities, such as the Treo 600. SoundRec supports one-touch recording and exporting to *.wav* files and the ability to adjust the recording quality (and how much memory the recordings take).

Hardware Solutions

If you want a hardware solution, then you have two choices: get a voice recorder stylus [Hack #51] or find a Palm III or equivalent [Hack #50]. For the Palm III solution, you will also need to locate a device called goVox—the tips for finding a cheap Palm apply equally well to finding a goVox. The goVox is a hardware voice recorder that hooks into a Palm III-class device.

Hacking the Hack

Personal Audio Recorder stores its memos in the Audio folder on your memory card as *.wav* files. Some music players may be able to play this format directly. For others, you can copy the files to the desktop, convert them from *.wav* into a more widely recognized format (*.mp3* or *.ogg*) and copy them back to your memory card. This allows you to play the voice memos using a music player instead of the voice memo application. Thus, you can listen to all of your voice memos back-to-back, or you can create play lists containing specific sets of memos.

Take Great Pictures with Your Palm

HACK #27

Anyone can point and shoot, but how do you get really memorable pictures with your Palm or Treo? This hack provides some simple tips to make your digital photos more interesting.

A camera phone doesn't have the resolution of a film camera or a regular digital camera. If you are planning on taking a lot of pictures, then you probably have a real camera with you. So that implies that camera phone pictures are going to happen on the spur of the moment. Understanding this is the key to getting good pictures. You need to develop the habits of watching for good photo opportunities and remembering that you always have your camera phone with you.

With that attitude in mind, here are some tips.

Framing

A shot is more interesting if it is framed. A person leaning against the support of a bridge is more interesting if you use the support as one edge of the picture. Frames are strong vertical or horizontal lines. Look for natural frames—buildings, trees, poles, or mountains. If your device supports it, zoom in or out to improve the framing.

Action

Movement is good and not usually something that you can set up for. Being quick with your phone can catch an action shot that you might not be able to get with a film camera.

Three Shots

If you have the time, snap off three slightly different shots of the same scene. Change your angle, view, framing, or zoom. With a digital camera, you can review the shots when you have a moment and just keep the best.

Change Your view

Want an unusual shot? Try climbing up and shooting down from a slight angle. Or lie down on the ground and aim up at the scene. Different angles can create interesting pictures. You can also try moving in for an extreme close-up.

Sometimes glare can be a problem. If you tilt your Palm device forward or backward slightly, then sometimes you can get the glare to go away. A very slight angle can make a big difference in removing glare without noticeably altering the picture you want to take. If tilting the camera doesn't work, then you may have to settle for taking the picture from a different angle.

Hacking the Hack

Frustrated by the limited resolution of your camera? You can take multiple pictures to increase the resolution of your camera. You can take a series of pictures panning left to right and stitch them together with an ordinary graphics program. There are also specialized programs for creating panoramic pictures out of a series of shots. One open-source example is Hugin (*http://hugin.sourceforge.net*) which is a graphical front end for the open-source program Panorama Tools (*http://www.path.unimelb.edu.au/~dersch/*). You can see Hugin in action in Figure 4-16. You can see what a typical output image looks like in Figure 4-17.

Even if you can't take perfect pictures every time, you can sometimes clean up your mistakes. If you're on a Mac, Apple's iPhoto has some decent photo touch-up features. Mac, Windows, and Linux users can also use the GIMP (*http://www.gimp.org*) to do extensive work with photos.

For more information on taking great photos, see *Digital Photography Hacks* (O'Reilly, 2004) and *Digital Photography: Expert Techniques* (O'Reilly, 2004). For specific information on panoramic photos, see *Assembling Panoramic Photos* (O'Reilly, 2005).

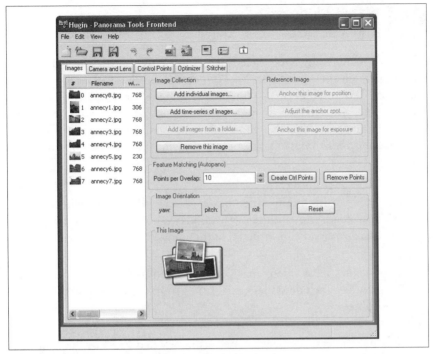

Figure 4-16. Hugin—getting ready to stitch photos together

Figure 4-17. Panoramic castle photo

Watch Videos

#28   Palm devices can display scaled-down videos—entertainment on the go!

There are many sources of legal videos on the Web. Most recent movies have trailers on their web sites. You can download these and view them on your Palm device. You can also find amateur videos on a variety of subjects. For example, you can find amateur Star Wars videos at *http://www.theforce. net*. I particularly like the short film Troops (*http://www.theforce.net/ fanfilms/shortfilms/troops/*). You can also find videos from a number of other sources:

Video software player sites
> The sites for the various video players usually have short clips that you can download. Most of the software plays the same types of videos, so you can download clips from all of the sites.

Games
> Many games have videos that you can download from their web sites. These videos include trailers, cut-scenes from the game, and player-created content.

Machinima
> This term refers to videos created using a video game as the source. If you search around the web, you can find sites for this such as *http:// www.machinima.com*.

Convert your own
> With the right conversion software, you can convert movies that you've purchased into a format that you can play back on your Palm.

Setting up Your Palm and PC

In addition to actually having some videos to download to your Palm, you need a few more things.

First, you need to have a memory card for your Palm device. For a Sony Clié, that means you need a Memory Stick or Memory Stick Pro. For a Palm-branded device, you need an SD or MMC card. Pick a card that will hold as many videos as you want to carry with you, plus has enough space for anything else (like music) that you might want. Even more than with songs, a number of variables affect playback of videos and the size of the files. There are encoding factors such as the number of frames per second, the size of the frames, and the length of the original video.

As with music, if you have a card reader for your PC, you can save lots of time by using it. Install videos in the folder */Video*.

Sony Clié

The next thing you need to do is install software on your PC to support transferring videos to the card on your Clié. This program is called Data Export. If you didn't install it when you initially installed the Palm Desktop software, then you will need to install it now off of the original CD.

Your PDA should already have the Data Import application installed. If not, then you will need to install it from the original CD as well.

The next step is to use the Data Export (PC side) and Data Import (PDA side) programs to transfer the videos you want to watch to the memory card in your PDA.

Palm-Branded Device

To transfer videos to an SD card on a Palm-branded device, you will use the Quick Install program from the Palm Desktop software. Then you just do a normal HotSync to transfer the files.

Conversion Software

You may also need some software for your PC to convert movie files to an appropriate image size and frame rate.

VirtualDub. VirtualDub *(http://www.virtualdub.org)* is an open-source program that allows you to convert videos from and to different formats, frame rates, and image sizes. It uses plug-ins for converting between *mpeg* and *avi* files.

DivX. DivX *(http://www.divx.com)* is a converter for the DivX format which works with VirtualDub. It is a free download. This site also sells a program called Dr. DivX, which is similar to VirtualDub.

LAME. LAME *(http://www.free-codecs.com/download/Lame_Encoder.htm)* is an MP3 codec for converting audio formats. LAME can be used with VirtualDub.

XviD. XviD *(http://www.xvid.org)* is an open-source MPEG encoder. It can be used with VirtualDub as well.

Palm Playback Software

You will also need some software for your Palm device to actually display the videos that you download and convert.

MMPlayer. MMPlayer [Hack #25] (*http://www.mmplayer.com*) allows you to play videos and music. With compression and conversion software, it is possible to compress a two hour movie onto a 128 MB memory card.

Kinoma Player. This player (*http://www.kinoma.com*) lets you watch videos, listen to music, and view JPEG images.

Pocket-DVD Studio. This player (*http://www.pqdvd.com*) lets you watch MPEG movies on your Palm device.

All of the programs should automatically detect and list files from the memory card.

You can watch movies using the built-in speaker, but the sound quality will be better (and you won't disturb the people around you) if you use headphones. I would recommend headphones that have their own volume control so you won't have to interrupt the movie to change the volume. The web site *http://www.headphone.com* has more information on headphones.

Treo
Hacks 29–33

The other chapters in this book cover the PDA functions of a Treo (or other Palm device) in great detail. This chapter focuses on the phone features that are specific to Treos.

The combination of a full-featured PDA with a cell phone enables you to do things that you can't do with either one alone. Smartphones really are the future of PDAs and cell phones. As the technology improves, there will be better integration of features and eventually higher data transfer speeds. For now, this chapter helps you smooth out some of the inevitable rough spots.

The Treo combines many of the PDA and phone features nicely. These hacks cover the gaps for things like ringtones and voice dialing. You will also learn about specialized Treo functions such as using your Treo as a modem or participating in conferences on the move. You also learn how to set up a master application that will help you get the most out of your Treo.

HACK #29 Take Charge of Ringtones

Set up your own ringtones on your Treo and skip the part where you pay your wireless provider lots of money.

Picking a ringtone can be a very emotional process, as it is perhaps the most defining personalization you can make to your Treo. You've probably already come across the Sound preference panel for the Phone application, as shown in Figure 5-1. And you probably were as disappointed as I was to realize that your choices are limited to the MIDI Ring Tones database, which contain cheesy MIDI sound files. You'd expect a little more from a $600 smartphone, like the ability to play MP3 or WAV files. The bad news is that you pretty much have to purchase an aftermarket application to do this, which can set you back $20 to $35, and will eat up about 700 KB of RAM on your Treo. The good news is that things work really well once you've made this investment.

The Treo 650 (but not the 600) has built-in support for a voice compression format: AMR on GSM Treos, and QCELP on CDMA Treos. For example, if you use the voice recorder to record yourself, the recording will be stored internally as AMR/QCELP, and will show up in the MIDI Ring Tones database. Then you can then select it as a ringtone in the Sound preference panel.

Figure 5-1. Using the built-in ringtones in the Preferences panel

Converting Sound Files

If you don't mind the very poor sound quality, it is possible to convert a WAV or MP3 sound file into the Treo 650's ARM/QCELP format, which will cause it to show up in the MIDI Ring Tones database for you to select as well. Here is the no-cost way of getting WAVs and MP3s as ringtones:

1. On your desktop or laptop computer, convert your desired sound file into a mono 8khz WAV file. (WinAmp, available from *http://www. winamp.com/*, should be able to do this.)

2. Get the WAV into your Treo 650 using one of the following techniques, which will automatically convert it to the ARM/QCELP format, causing it to show up in your MIDI Ring Tone database:

   a. Email this WAV file to your Palm, and open the attachment in Versamail.

   b. If your desktop has Bluetooth or Infrared, send it via Bluetooth or beam it via Infrared to your Treo 650.

   c. Store the file in a directory in an expansion card, and insert it into your Treo 650. Then enter its URL in your web browser; hit Go to add it to the MIDI Ring Tone database. Use a URL like **file:///** **directory/yourmidifile.mid**.

3. Select the converted sound file from the MIDI Ring Tone database using the Sound Preferences panel.

There are a handful of programs that are designed to play WAV and MP3 files as ringtones on your Treo, though some work better than others. The de facto standard these days seems to be ToySoft's LightWav 5 (*http://www. toysoft.ca*), which has a 14-day trial; after that, you pay $19.95 to register it. LightWav 5 has lots of cool features, like the ability to play an animated GIF while the phone is ringing, assigning video or images to caller ID, blocking calls and SMS messages from particular caller IDs, and so forth. But most importantly, LightWav will let you assign a WAV, MP3, or OGG file as a ringtone!

> If you wish to play files compressed in the MP3 or OGG format, LightWav requires that you *also* have PocketTunes installed to decompress them (Pocket Tunes *is not necessary* if you just want to play WAV files, which are not compressed). PocketTunes has a 15-day free trial and then costs $14.95 from *http://www.normsoft.com*. If you've never used PocketTunes, it is an excellent music player that is able to play sounds in the background while you use your Treo for other things. With PocketTunes and a large-capacity expansion card, your Treo becomes an excellent personal music device **[Hack #25]**; for this reason, PocketTunes should be on any Treo user's short list of must-have applications.

LightWav will let you use sound files on your expansion card, but it will also let you move those sounds into your Treo's RAM if you wish. That way, even if you take your expansion card out, LightWav will still be able to find your custom ringtones when it needs to play them.

Installing Ringtones

First, load up your expansion card with MP3, WAV, or OGG sound clips you want to use and insert it into your Treo. Be sure the sound clips go into the */audio* directory—the Palm Install Tool will do this by default. Launch LightWav, select the item to which you wish to assign a custom sound from the list, and then select Edit from the context menu that pops up. Figure 5-2 shows how to modify the Known Caller ringtone using the Edit option.

From the Edit Ringer screen, ensure you've checked the Enable Ringer checkbox, as shown in Figure 5-3.

Tap on Select ringtone, and you should see a list of the ringtones in the supported format on your expansion card, which is shown in Figure 5-4. If you aren't seeing your MP3 or OGG files, make sure you have PocketTunes installed. Notice the *Cvt* button, which is what you can use to convert the selected sound file into your Treo's RAM, so that you don't need to have the expansion card inserted to play it.

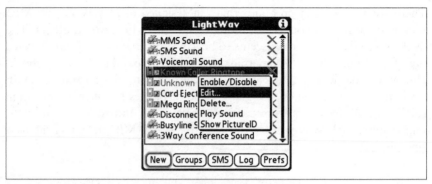

Figure 5-2. Editing the Known Caller ringtone in LightWav

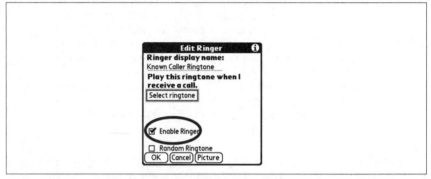

Figure 5-3. Don't forget to Enable Ringer in the Edit Ringer screen!

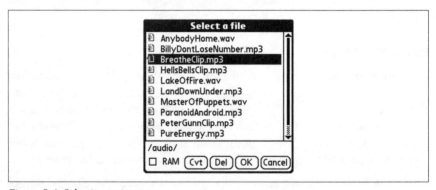

Figure 5-4. Selecting a ringtone

One last step and you're done. To prevent the Treo's built-in MIDI ringtone from playing on top of the LightWav sound file, you must disable the tones in your Sound Preferences panel, as Figure 5-5 shows.

That's all there is to customizing ringtones. Have fun personalizing your Treo!

—Jeff Ishaq

Figure 5-5. Setting the Known and Unknown caller tones to Silent

 Dial with Your Voice

Use your voice instead of your fingers to dial your Treo. This can be useful if your hands are occupied.

You might not see the need for voice dialing until you've tried to dial a contact while driving. Even if you're very familiar with navigating your contacts single-handedly, you still have to glance at the keypad from time to time. With voice dialing, it becomes much easier and safer to perform this task. Most cell phones come with some kind of voice dialing system as a standard feature, and most generally follow the same sequence to dial a contact:

1. Push a button to put the phone into listen mode, as seen in Figure 5-6.

2. Speak the name of the contact you wish to dial into the phone, which attempts to translate what you've spoken into a known contact.

3. The verification phase, which is typically optional, though on by default, will cause the phone to speak the matching contact's name (if a match was found) back to you, so you are sure it's calling the right person, as Figure 5-7 shows. You will have the option to cancel the call if necessary; for example, sometimes "Lab" might be recognized in error by the phone as "Dad," so this verification step prevents you from calling the wrong contact.

4. The contact is dialed.

Strangely, however, neither the Treo 600 nor the Treo 650 comes with built-in voice dialing, despite this feature being one of the top customer requests. You do have options, though none are free. Table 5-1 shows a breakdown of the most popular voice dialing options.

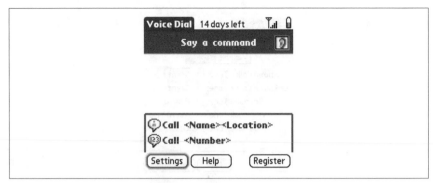

Figure 5-6. Palm's Treo Voice Dialing is listening for your voice

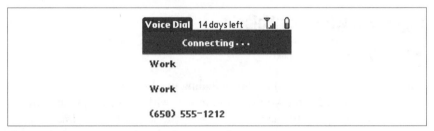

Figure 5-7. Treo Voice Dialing verifies its match on-screen

Table 5-1. Voice dialing options

System	Price	Notes
Treo Voice Dialing by Voice-Signal, available under *www.palm.com* Support Downloads for the Treo 650	14-day free trial; then, $19.95 buys a registration key	No voice training required
		Not available for Treo 600
		Not compatible with GoodLinka software
		Use voice commands to launch applications, etc
Voice Dialer by Voicelt Technologies, LLC, available from *http://www.voiceit-tech.com*	10-day free trial; then, get a registration key for $24.95 for the standard version, and $34.95 for pro version	Works with Treo 650 and Treo 600
		Voice training is required for each contact
		Pro version also lets you train voice commands to launch applications, etc.
Sprint PCS Voice Command, a feature you can add to your Sprint plan online or by calling 1-888-253-1315	You can usually talk them into giving you a 2-month free trial; then it's $5/mo	No voice training required
		Works for any and all phones under the plan
		Must upload your contacts to Sprint
		Not available when roaming

a GoodLink is a very popular and extremely powerful system for accessing a Microsoft Exchange server over your Treo's wireless Internet connection

Here's the bottom line for voice dialing on your Treo. If you have a Treo 650, you are best off with Treo Voice Dialing, which Palm.com distributes for VoiceSignal. It has received very good reviews, and no training is required, meaning you don't have to record yourself saying all of your contacts' names. Rather, the software is sophisticated enough to figure out what you're saying. The only flaw is that it is not compatible with GoodLink.

If you have a Treo 600 like I do, or you have a Treo 650 and GoodLink, then Voice Dialer is your best bet. While it does require you to record yourself saying each of your contacts' names that you wish to voice-dial, once you get it set up, it works very well and you'll wonder how you lived without it.

I wouldn't waste money on Sprint PCS Voice Command. Though it does work for *all* the phones under one Sprint plan, it's still $5 a month until the end of time—which is certainly more expensive than a one-time payment to buy the registration key for the other two options. Also, if you are roaming, you won't have access to voice commands, which is the deal-breaker for me.

—*Jeff Ishaq*

H A C K

#31
Use Your Treo as a Modem

Use your Treo to connect your laptop to the Internet. You can also use your Treo as a backup Internet connection for your desktop machine.

If you've signed up for your carrier's wireless data plan, you can get the *entire* Internet on your Treo. It may not seem like it at times, because the small screen can really constrain your web-browsing experience when compared to, say, your laptop or your desktop computer, but it's all there—every last byte. Better still, it is possible to feed the Internet connection of your Treo through to your laptop computer. This is called *tethering*, and it allows your tethered laptop to work with the Internet as if it were connected via a normal dial-up, cable, or DSL modem—only, you are connected using your Treo. Anywhere your Treo has enough signal strength to connect to its wireless data service, you can tether it to supply a laptop with Internet.

> You can also channel your Treo's Internet connection through your computer [Hack #34] if you wish. Though it's not as convenient as using your Treo as a modem, it does come in handy if your desktop's Internet connection happens to be down.

Setting up tethering is specific to the model of your Treo and your cellular service provider and is summed up in Table 5-2. You use either your Treo 650's Bluetooth connectivity to use the Treo as a wireless modem for your laptop or desktop, or you need a third-party Windows application called PdaNet, which allows you to connect your Treo (as a modem) to your laptop or desktop via the USB sync cable.

 Tethering might be frowned upon by your carrier. Carriers will argue that tethering is abusing a network infrastructure that is set up in anticipation of the light bandwidth consumption of average smartphone users. Power users will argue that when paying $45 per month for "unlimited Internet," you are entitled to get that for which you've paid. So it's important that you become familiar with your service provider's policy on tethering if you plan to use it frequently—you may be surprised.

Table 5-2. Wireless providers

Device	Carrier	Tethering technique
Treo 650	Sprint	Built-in Bluetooth DUN is now supported, provided you apply the "Treo 650 Updater 1.12 for Sprint PCS," found at *http://www.palm.com/us/support/downloads/treo650updater/sprint.html*.
		You may also use PdaNet for tethering over your USB sync cable or wirelessly over Bluetooth.
	Verizon and other CDMA carriers (e.g., EarthLink)	Built-in Bluetooth DUN is *not* supported, and no firmware update is promised.
		Hack your device to enable Bluetooth DUN now, without waiting for Verizon's firmware update. The hack is fairly stable.
		You may also use PdaNet for tethering over your USB sync cable or wirelessly over Bluetooth.
	Cingular and other GSM carriers (e.g., AT&T Wireless, Rogers)	Built-in Bluetooth DUN is *not* supported. Cingular promises a firmware update "later this year," according to a Palm support page dated March 31, 2005.
		Hack your device to enable Bluetooth DUN now, without waiting for a firmware update. The hack is fairly stable.
		You may also use PdaNet for tethering over your USB sync cable or wirelessly over Bluetooth (no hack required).
Treo 600	All	This device does not support Bluetooth. Your only option is to use PdaNet for tethering over your USB sync cable.

Treo 650 Bluetooth DUN

To enable Bluetooth DUN on your Treo 650:

1. Run the Bluetooth application.

2. Enable the Dial-up Networking settings, as shown in Figure 5-8 (if you don't see this setting, you need to check for a firmware update for your Treo 650, or apply the shadowmite patch—see the sidebar "The 'shadowmite' Patch").

Figure 5-8. Turning on the Dial-up Networking setting on a Treo 650

The "shadowmite" Patch

The Treo 650 Bluetooth DUN hack, also called the "shadowmite" patch after the handle of the developer who discovered it, exposes the Dial-up Networking setting in the Bluetooth preferences panel for those devices that don't already show it. For various reasons (some say political—remember, some carriers would rather you didn't know about tethering), Palm disabled this DUN setting at the last minute before shipping the Treo 650 device. That means that hacking this setting to appear and subsequently enabling it is certainly *not* going to be supported by the technical support departments of Palm or your carrier! The good news is that the shadowmite patch appears stable, it's totally reversible (to un-patch, simply delete the patch file), many people are using it without incident, and there's an online forum where you can post questions. *Before* you go this route, make sure that your carrier hasn't already released a firmware update that enables DUN support (as Sprint has)! For more information on the shadowmite patch, including the patch itself, visit *http://www.shadowmite.com/HowToDUN.html*.

The steps in getting Bluetooth DUN set up on your laptop (or desktop) varies with operating system and Bluetooth hardware—please consult your manuals for help here. But in general, you want to do something like this:

1. Make sure your Treo is on and Bluetooth has been enabled.

2. Open the Bluetooth control panel/system preferences on your laptop (or desktop).

3. If you area PC user, your Treo 650 should be discovered. If you are a Mac user, set up a new Mobile Phone device.

4. Establish a connection between your laptop and your Treo 650.

5. Look for your Treo 650's Dial Up Networking service on your laptop; if you only see its Object Exchange service, try performing a soft reset on your Treo 650.

6. Create a dial-up connection to your Treo 650's Dial Up Networking service on your laptop. See Table 5-3 for the values that should work for you. A quick phone call to your carrier can get you going if these don't work.

Table 5-3. Carrier data connection information

Carrier	Username	Password	Phone number
Sprint	*YourSprintPCSVisionUsername@sprintpcs.com* (you may not need the "@sprintpcs.com" part)	*YourSprintPCSVision Password*	#777
Verizon	*YourPhoneNumber* @vzw3g.com	vzw	#777
Cingular	*WAP@CINGULARGPRS.COM*	CINGULAR1	**99***1#
T-Mobile	none	none	*99#

PdaNet

You can download the PdaNet application from June Fabrics PDA Technology Group at *http://www.junefabrics.com/*. It has a 15-day trial, after which the application costs $34 to register to your Treo device.

For Treo 600 users with a Mac, the picture is grim. (Treo 650 users with a Mac should opt to use the Bluetooth technique described earlier.) PdaNet suggests it can run under Virtual PC, though that only gives your emulated PC access to the Internet—and this usage is not supported. There is also WirelessModem, which you can download from *http://www.notifymail.com/palm/wmodem/*. It has a 14-day free trial; then it's $37.50 to register the application. Be very careful with this application; many users are unable to maintain an Internet connection to their Mac for more than five minutes, and there is no return policy.

There is a great guide to connecting your Treo 650 to a Mac using Bluetooth at *http://vocaro.com/trevor/treo-dun/*.

Once you've downloaded and run the installer for your specific Treo model (check carefully!), you are prompted to select the appropriate cell phone service from the screen in Figure 5-9.

Figure 5-9. Selecting your carrier in PdaNet's installer

The Windows component is installed to your desktop, and then you are prompted to HotSync the Palm component onto your Treo (see Figure 5-10).

Once the installation is complete, you will notice a new PdaNet icon in your System Tray (the icons by your clock), which indicates your connection status, as shown in Figure 5-11.

The PdaNet icon indicates whether you have an active Internet connection through your Treo; right-click on it to get to the advanced PdaNet settings.

After you've installed the PdaNet application onto your Treo, make sure your device is connected to your laptop with a USB HotSync cable (serial HotSync cables will not work), and then simply launch the PdaNet application on your Treo. Figure 5-12 shows PdaNet running on a Treo.

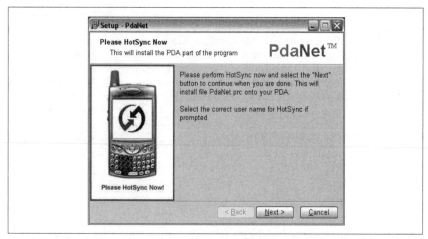

Figure 5-10. PdaNet's installer queues up a PRC to install onto your Treo

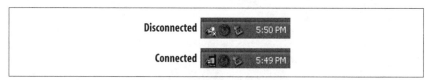

Figure 5-11. PdaNet's icon indicates a connected or disconnected state

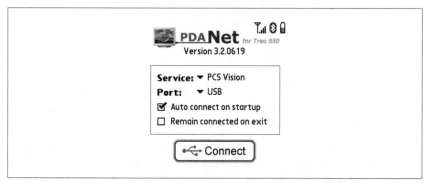

Figure 5-12. PdaNet is ready to connect your laptop to the Internet

Your Treo automatically attempts to establish a connection to its wireless Internet service, and if successful, PdaNet will then tether that connection over your USB HotSync cable to your laptop. Figure 5-13 show PdaNet's desktop component confirming its Internet connectivity.

You should now be able to use any Internet applications on your laptop, as long as your Treo is able to keep connected to its wireless Internet service. Be sure to disconnect your Treo when you're done!

Figure 5-13. After your Treo connects to its wireless data network, the Windows component tethers to it

 Though some service providers' wireless data plans offer unlimited usage, most allot a certain number of kilobytes per month and will charge you a fortune for overages. Check into this before you consume too many KB on your Treo.

—Jeff Ishaq

 ## HACK #32 Join Conferences on the Move

If you have your Treo with you, you can participate in conferences anywhere. With a few simple techniques, you can feel as if you are in the room with everyone else.

The basic idea for conferencing is to combine a phone call with either a web session or a VNC session.

Web Presentation

If the conference call is basically some sort of presentation, then it is trivial to get set up. The presenter makes the presentation available over the Web (on a secure web site if needed). You can download the document from the Web and save it to your Treo before you switch to the phone, as you can see in Figure 5-14.

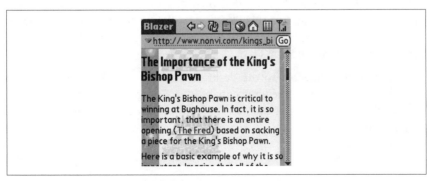

Figure 5-14. Viewing a downloaded document

Use your standard voice conferencing (or just call the conference room if you are the only one calling in). After you have called in, switch back to the web browser to view the document that you downloaded. That way, you can follow along during the presentation.

VNC Conference

The web presentation method works well when information is mostly going one way (e.g., for a presentation). It doesn't work as well when you need to collaborate or work interactively. A method that allows for collaboration is to use VNC [Hack #40]. This method requires that you be able to access the Internet while having a phone call active. A recent patch allows Sprint Treos to use Bluetooth to access the Internet while on a phone call. You can use this (or an equivalent patch for other providers, as they become available) to run PalmVNC. You see a desktop example of VNC in Figure 5-15.

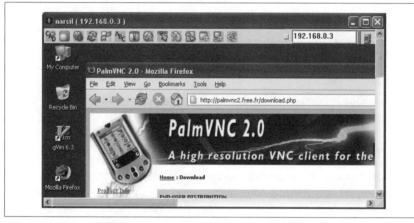

Figure 5-15. Sharing desktops in VNC

UltraVNC (*http://www.ultravnc.com*) provides a chat capability, as you see in Figure 5-16. You can use this to communicate instead of using a phone. This allows you to use VNC even if you can't connect to the Internet while making a phone call on your Treo.

After you have connected to the desktop machine with VNC, then call in using your standard conferencing capabilities. This sort of conference works best if someone is sitting at the desktop computer that is acting as the VNC server. This person can easily launch programs and open documents that everyone else can see.

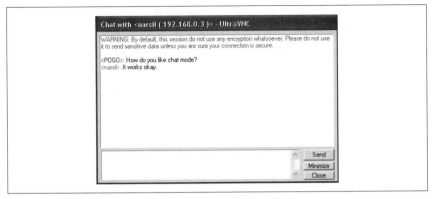

Figure 5-16. Chat window in UltraVNC

WebEx

WebEx (*http://www.webex.com*) provides a web-based sharing capability. One computer acts as the host for a meeting, somewhat similar to VNC, except you have to explicitly share applications in WebEx. WebEx has native clients for Windows, Linux, Palm, and Mac. You will need to be able to browse the Web while a phone call is active, as with VNC conferencing.

You can use your regular phone conferencing setup while using WebEx to share applications. If you are looking for a phone conferencing capability, WebEx also provides phone conferencing.

HACK #33

Set Up a Master Application

Depending on how you primarily use your Treo, you can set up different applications to be your master (or primary) application. This involves configuring your chosen application to provide easy access to the Treo's other functions.

Someone who uses a Treo mostly as a cell phone should have a different setup than someone who mostly uses the organizer features. If you have a Treo, however, you presumably want to make some use of all the categories of features: phone, organizer, and Internet access. This hack will help you to optimize your Treo for your preferred application while also providing convenient access to the other features. Each section covers optimizing for a specific application.

There are a few general strategies which apply to all applications. The goal of these optimizations is to provide quick access to the things you do most often and slightly less convenient access to the things you do less frequently.

(By the way, this is a fundamental principle that professional user interface designers use when designing software or electronic devices.)

The easiest access comes from the hardware buttons that turn on the Treo and open an application all at one time—the Phone, Date Book, and Messaging buttons. Next in convenience are single buttons or single taps from within an open application. After that are multiple key combinations (e.g., Option and another button), multiple taps on the screen, and combinations of buttons and taps.

One decision you will need to make for yourself is whether you prefer hardware buttons (including the 5-way navigator) or whether you prefer tapping with the stylus. This may influence how you set up shortcuts between applications.

The first step for any type of application is to set up a hardware button to launch it [Hack #44]. If one of the default buttons already launches your preferred application with a single touch, then you might as well use that button. Otherwise, hold your Treo in one hand, as you normally would when using it. Figure out which button is more convenient for you—the Date Book or the Messaging—and set that button to launch your chosen application. It might be a good idea to leave the phone button set to launch the Phone application.

Phone

The Phone application is very powerful. If you use your Treo primarily as a phone, then this is a good choice for your master application. You can set both the Date Book and Messaging buttons to launch secondary applications.

In addition to dialing phone numbers from either the keyboard or the dial pad, you can also launch other applications from the Phone application, as you can see in Figure 5-17. If you choose to view appointments on the main Phone screen (General Preferences → Show Calendar event), then you can switch to the Date Book with a single-tap or via the 5-way navigator. All you have to do is tap on the appointment line on the screen, or highlight it with the 5-way navigator and hit the center button. This will open the Date Book to the Daily view for the current day.

The Phone application provides access to other applications via the Favorites buttons. These buttons can be set to speed dial a phone number, create a new email to a given email address, open a particular web page, or open an arbitrary application. You can have 0 to 7 rows of favorites. You can only have one row if you want the dial pad visible (for tapping out phone

Figure 5-17. Phone application with access to three other applications

numbers) or two rows if you hide the appointment line. To get more than that, you have to hide the dial pad (General Preferences → Show Wallpaper instead of Show Dial Pad).

You can access a full page of favorites by pressing the down direction on the 5-way navigator. You can use the navigator to switch between favorites (center button to activate), or you can switch between five different pages of favorites using controls on the Favorites page.

Each favorite can have a key assigned to it. A key can only be assigned to one function. To activate a favorite via its hotkey, press and hold the key. Also, you can choose to have typing on the keyboard start dialing a phone number or start a lookup in your contacts. In the Phone application, under General Preferences, you can choose either *Typing starts dialing phone number* or *Typing starts Contacts search*. If the keyboard is set to dial a phone number, then the keyboard behaves as if the Option key has been pressed for all keys. Otherwise, the keyboard behaves normally.

Date Book

If you primarily use your Treo to organize your time, then you can use the Date Book as your master application. You see an example in Figure 5-18 in which you can get to the To Do list and email by tapping on the appropriate section of the screen. If you want to be able to dial phone numbers directly from an appointment or a To Do item, then you will need to replace the built-in PIM applications with a third-party application such as Agendus (*http://www.iambic.com*). With a third-party application installed you can add phone numbers to scheduled appointments. Selecting the phone number allows you to dial it directly. If you don't have a third-party application installed, then you need to copy the phone number from the appointment (or To Do item) and paste it into the Phone application.

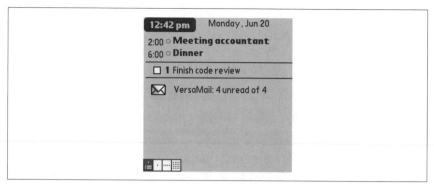

Figure 5-18. Date Book showing Today view

When creating an appointment, use the Phone Lookup feature from the Edit menu to add the appropriate phone number.

Contacts

The Contacts application lets you easily make calls by creating a specific category for frequently called numbers. The standard name on Palm devices for this category is QuickList, but you should pick something that makes sense to you. If you start the category name with a space, it will appear first in the list of categories, making it easier to get to. If you keep your frequently-called list short enough that it all fits on screen, then you can access the numbers with a single tap. Hold down the space bar when you have a contact highlighted to pop up a list of all the numbers for that contact. After you choose a number, press the center button to dial it.

As with the Date Book, if you want direct access to email or web sites from your contacts application, then you will need to find a third-party application. If you do install a third-party application, then you can create categories like Email and Web Sites that just contain the corresponding data. These categories can act like favorites or bookmarks.

Web

You can use the web browser as your master application. This may be a good choice if you primarily use your Treo for Internet access. From the browser, select phone numbers and hit the center button to dial them, or select email addresses and press the center button to create a new email message. You can also use the Internet to look up phone numbers for businesses or people and dial directly from the web page, as in Figure 5-19.

Figure 5-19. Dialing a number from a web page

To use the browser as your master application, you should create a web page with contact information on it. You can create internal navigation links at the top of the page—maybe sections like Business or Personal. List each person's name and contact information (phone or email). Download this page to your browser, then save it locally on your Treo. Make a hotkey for this page. Then, whenever you need to make a call or send an email, just bring up this saved page, select the appropriate data, and press the center button.

## CHAPTER SIX

Communications
Hacks 34–41

With the introduction of wireless technologies (Bluetooth, Wi-Fi, cellular) into Palm devices, a whole range of new applications opened up. Even with these newer technologies, some vintage applications still work with the serial or infrared port.

The hacks in this chapter cover a range of ideas from connecting to the Internet to controlling your home theater. As wireless transfer speeds increase in the future, you will see more possibilities open up. You will also see merging of different applications—using voice and data transfers together at the same time.

Communications weaves through other areas as well. Multiplayer games depend on different communications technologies. Collecting information for use in other applications is easier with improved communications technology (e.g., browsing the Web), as is transferring that information to other people.

As communications technology changes in the future, the chances are good that Palm devices will adapt as well.

Connect to the Internet

#34 Just because you aren't at your desktop machine, it doesn't mean you have to be disconnected. Depending on your PDA, you have several different choices for getting on the Internet.

All Palm devices can connect to the Internet via modem or serial cable and most can connect via infrared (IR). Bluetooth-equipped Palm devices can connect via Bluetooth. Other options for connecting to the Internet include Wi-Fi (802.11b) and using your cellular data service on a smartphone.

Modem

You can purchase a regular modem for most Palm devices that connects to a standard phone line. For older devices, you might need to look on eBay (*http://www.ebay.com*) or at a computer swap meet to find a modem.

Configuring your Palm device to use a modem is easy. Go to the Preferences application and select the Network category. Select your service and enter your username and password. Select Standard Modem in the Connection list. Enter the phone number for your ISP. The Details button brings up a dialog box that lets you select additional options—connection type (defaults to PPP, but you can choose SLIP or CSLIP if necessary), an idle timeout that will hang up after a specified period of inactivity, whether or not to do DNS queries automatically, and whether to use a static IP address or a dynamic address. The dialog box also provides the ability to write a simple script. You can use this to automate certain tasks.

Set additional parameters for a modem by selecting Edit Connections from the connection list. Select a connection from the dialog box, and then press the Edit button. Then you will be able to modify settings such as what you are connecting to (PC, modem, or LAN) and whether you are connecting via cable or IR. Also, you can choose between TouchTone and rotary dialing, and set the volume for dialing and connecting. If you select Details, you can set the speed of the connection, the type of flow control, and any initialization string.

Serial Cable or Cradle

Setting up a connection via a serial cable or cradle is similar to setting up a modem, except that you don't have to enter a phone number, username, or password. Choose Cradle / Cable from the Connection list. Note that you need to be running a PPP stack on your desktop machine to connect via cable. For Windows machines, you can get a PPP stack called SoftickPPP (*http://www.softick.com/ppp/*). This stack supports USB, Serial, Infrared, and Bluetooth connections. Configuring Softick PPP is fairly simple, as you can see in Figure 6-1.

The one tricky setting depends on what kind of device you have. For Sony Cliés (and some other devices—check the Softick web site for more details), you will need to set the PPP stack to operate in *exclusive mode*. This means that you can't HotSync while connecting to the Internet. Most devices can do this, but for the ones that can't, you need to select Use USB in exclusive mode from the USB tab in PPP, as you can see in Figure 6-2. You will need to enable Softick PPP explicitly when you want to connect to the Internet and disable it when you want to HotSync.

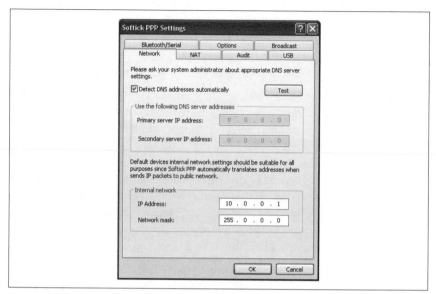

Figure 6-1. Setting up Softick PPP on Windows

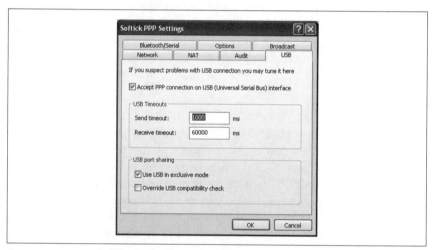

Figure 6-2. Setting Softick PPP to use exclusive mode on the USB port

Another choice for connecting with a cable is to buy a cable to connect your Palm device to a cell phone. You can find cables online at various sites such as *http://www.thesupplynet.com*. Your cell phone must be set up with data access through your wireless service provider. A cell phone can act as a modem (follow the modem instructions) or as a direct network access point. You will need to check your wireless service plan for details.

You can also edit the connection (as with a modem) to select what you are connecting to.

Infrared (IR)

You can use an infrared connection to a desktop computer or to a cell phone. For a desktop computer, the setup is similar to setting up a connection through a serial cable, except that you will choose IR or IR to a PC/Handheld from the Connection list. Connecting to a phone depends on whether the phone acts as a modem or as a direct network access point. Check your service plan for details. Select the appropriate connection type—IR to a GSM Phone, if that is applicable, otherwise choose IR or IR to a PC/Handheld. If you are using the phone as a modem, then follow the modem instructions.

Bluetooth

You can connect to the Internet via Bluetooth, if your Palm device has it installed. If your Palm device doesn't have Bluetooth built-in, you may be able to buy an adapter [Hack #53], depending on which device you have.

You need a Bluetooth-enabled access point to get on the Internet. That can be an access point, a cell phone, or your desktop computer.

Bluetooth LAN access point. If you are connecting through a LAN Access Point (either your office or some other business like a coffee shop), then you will need to get the network information from them. If you are in a public place that has Bluetooth access, this information is usually posted somewhere convenient.

If you are connecting to an access point, select Trusted Devices and Add Device. Your Palm device will then search for Bluetooth access points. You may have to search more than once to find the network you are looking for.

When the network is found, tap on it and hit OK. You need to enter in a passkey—this is something that you set up when you were configuring your desktop, or it should be available from the provider of the access point.

Cell phone. You will need to find out from your cell phone service provider whether or not you have data service set up on your cell phone, and if so, how should you access it. Some cell phones can be used as modems [Hack #31]. Your wireless plan also needs to support this. Other plans will let you use your cell phone as a direct network access point. You need to make sure that your wireless plan allows you to connect other devices to your phone. This is usually called *tethering*.

If your phone and plan support it, then you can connect your Palm device to your phone. From the Bluetooth Preferences, select Setup Device. You will also probably want to set your Palm device to not be discoverable, unless you want people trying to connect to your Palm device.

From the Setup Devices form, select Phone Setup and then Phone Connection. Make sure your cell phone is set to be discoverable, select your phone model, and type in a passkey to pair the devices (as with a desktop connection). You will have to type the same passkey into your cell phone when prompted.

After you have paired the phone and your Palm device, your Palm device will ask you if you want to set up your device to connect to the Internet. Answer yes, and then follow the remaining prompts. When you are finished, go to Bluetooth Preferences and tap the Connect button to finally make the connection.

At this point, you should be able to access the Internet.

Use a Windows XP computer as an access point. If you are connecting through your desktop machine, you will also need a Bluetooth adapter on your desktop. Make sure that your drivers are up-to-date.

Start by making sure that Bluetooth is set up and working on both the PC and Palm. Then, create a COM port for the Bluetooth connection.

1. Double-click on the Bluetooth icon in the System Tray, and then click on the COM Ports tab. Click Add to add a new COM port. Select the *Incoming* option in the Add COM Port dialog box (as you can see in Figure 6-3), and then hit OK.

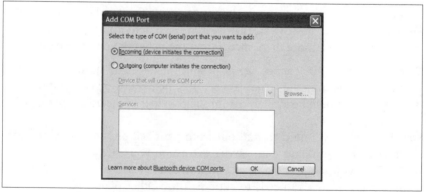

Figure 6-3. Setting up a COM port for Bluetooth in Windows XP

2. Windows will install the serial port. Wait a minute or so for it to finish up. When you return to the COM Ports tab of the Bluetooth settings dialog box, there should be a new COM port—in my case, it was COM7, as you see in Figure 6-4. Yours may be different, so write down what you see in your tab and click OK to close the dialog box.

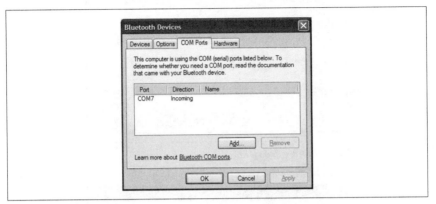

Figure 6-4. COM Ports tab in Windows Bluetooth setup dialog box

Now you need to create a modem that lives on this COM port.

1. Open the Control Panel and make your way to Phone and Modem options. You'll see a list of modems. Click Add to add a new modem.

2. From the Add Hardware Wizard, select *Don't detect my modem* and click Next.

3. You'll see a list of choices. If your system is similar to mine, the choice you need will be at or near the top. Choose (Standard Modem Types) under Manufacturer and choose *Communications cable between two computers* under Models, as you can see in Figure 6-5.

4. Click Next to proceed to the next screen, where you will select the COM port you created earlier (COM7 in my case). Click Next to move to the last screen and click Finish. You'll return to the Phone and Modem options control panel, where your new modem should appear, as in Figure 6-6.

Now you need to create the incoming PPP connection.

1. Start the New Connection Wizard (Click Start, Connect To, Show All Connections, and then choose New Connection from the File menu).

2. Use the following settings across the next few screens:

   a. Set up an advanced connection. Click Next.

   b. Accept incoming connections. Click Next.

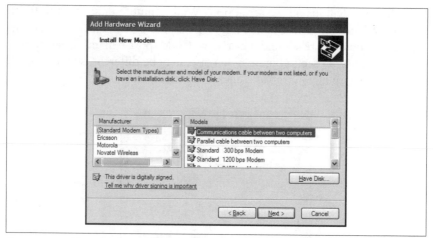

Figure 6-5. Add Hardware Wizard setup

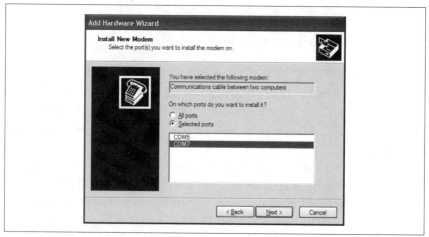

Figure 6-6. Control Panel showing new modem added

> c. Select Communications cable between two computers (COM7) as the connection device (the actual COM port should be the one you created earlier). Click Next.
>
> d. Do not allow virtual private network connections. Click Next.
>
> e. At this point, you should have a dialog box similar to Figure 6-7.

3. You need to choose a user, so *I suggest you* click Add to create a new user that will be dedicated to this connection. Name it **palm** and give it a password for security's sake, as in Figure 6-8. You are setting up a user that will be able to connect to your computer via Bluetooth, so all of the usual cautions about strong passwords apply here.

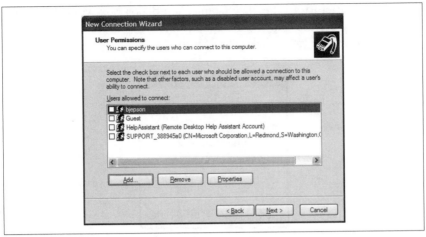

Figure 6-7. Selecting users to have access to Bluetooth

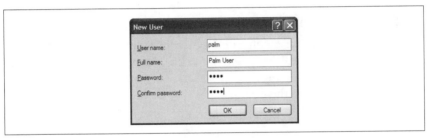

Figure 6-8. Adding a new user

4. Make sure palm is the only user selected and then complete the New Connection Wizard.

5. Make sure your Windows XP system is discoverable (double-click on the Bluetooth icon in the System tray, select the Options tag, Turn discovery on, and click OK).

Once the other side is set up and you have the connection information, you need to enable Bluetooth on your Palm device:

1. Run the Preferences application, select Communications, and tap Connection. Tap New to create a new connection.

2. Name the connection BT (or whatever you want) and specify that you will Connect to PC, Via Bluetooth. Click Tap to Find, which will initiate the Bluetooth discovery process.

3. Choose your PC from the list that results and perform the Bluetooth pairing. You shouldn't need to pair again once the devices have paired.

4. When you return to the New Connection dialog box, your PC's name should replace the Tap to Find button (my PC is called JEPSPIRON as shown in Figure 6-9). Click OK to finish.

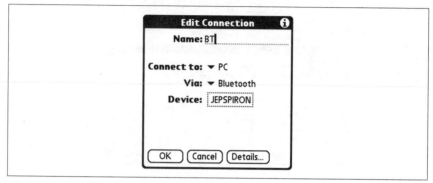

Figure 6-9. Editing a Bluetooth connection

Next, you need to create the Network connection.

1. From Preferences, selection Communications, and tap Network. Create a new connection called Bluetooth to PC (or whatever you want) that uses the Connection you created earlier. Specify the username and password you set up on the desktop side. The dialog box should look similar to Figure 6-10.

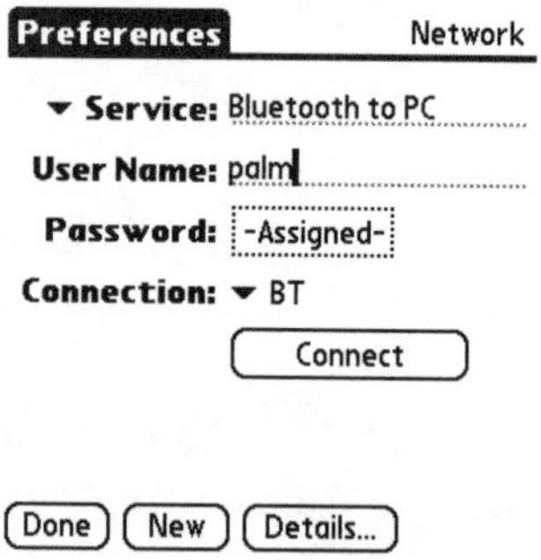

Figure 6-10. Setting up the Bluetooth network connection

2. Tap Details, and then tap Script. Set up the script as shown in Figure 6-11.

   • Send: **CLIENT**

   • Send: **CLIENT**

   • Wait For: **CLIENTSERVER**

Figure 6-11. Setting up a script for Bluetooth

3. Tap OK to return to the details page, and then tap OK again to return to the Network preferences. Tap Connect to make the connection. Once you are connected, select Options / View Log from the menu to see your connection details, as in Figure 6-12. You can also test the network connection from this screen by running the ping command.

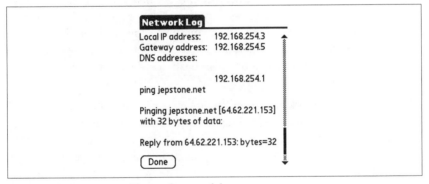

Figure 6-12. Examining a Bluetooth network log

Notice that the subnet of the local IP address (the Palm device) and of the Gateway Address (the desktop side) are the same. That's because the desktop isn't using Internet Connection Sharing (if it's a Windows box) which would normally set up a Network Address Translation (NAT) network. Instead, it puts your Palm device right on the same network as the desktop.

Troubleshooting. I hate to say it, but when I had problems connecting to my Windows XP box, the only solution that worked was to reboot the Windows machine.

Also, while you are connecting, you can press down on your Palm's five-way navigation pad. This will show you what the Palm is sending over the network, so you can get an idea of whether the Palm is even talking to anything.

Wi-Fi (802.11b)

Getting set up for Wi-Fi depends on whether 802.11b is built in (e.g., the Tungsten C) or whether 802.11b access is coming from an add-on card.

Setting up internal Wi-Fi. To get started with built-in Wi-Fi, select Wi-Fi Setup from the Palm Launcher. Tap Next and your Palm device will search for all available networks. If the application finds the network you want to connect to, then you are set—just tap the network name to continue.

If the network you were looking for was not found, then you need to tap the Other button. You will need to enter the network name (SSID) in the corresponding field. Finally, tap OK and Done, unless you want to set up a VPN first.

You can also configure WEP encryption. This will help make your connection more secure, but it is not guaranteed to be completely secure. When you enter the network name under Other, you have an option to turn on WEP encryption. You can also select this option by editing the network connection. If you check the WEP Encryption box, then you can set an encryption key. Tapping on the encryption key control brings up a dialog box with options for choosing a key type, specifying up to four keys, and also a key index that specifies which of the four keys to use. Set these as appropriate to match the network. The dialog box also has a text field for entering in your WEP keys. Tap OK when finished.

After the basic network has been set up, you can configure the standard Internet settings. Launch the Preferences application and select Wi-Fi. Select Edit Networks from the Network list and then choose the network you want to edit. Tap Details, then Advanced—it seems like all the interesting stuff is always hidden behind an Advanced button. The Advanced button brings up a dialog box that lets you choose between a static and dynamic IP address (and lets you configure the subnet mask and router for a dynamic address). You can also choose to use the default DNS server or to use a DNS server at a specific IP address.

Setting up a Wi-Fi card. Launch the Preferences application and select the Wi-Fi category. Select On in the list. The Wi-Fi card will automatically search for available networks. The Wi-Fi card will try to connect to the first network it finds. If you want to connect to a different network, then you need to tap on the Network list. If the network you want to connect to appears in the list, then go ahead and select it.

If the network does not appear in the list, you will need to set it up manually. Launch the Wi-Fi Setup application. Tap Next, and then tap Other to bring up a dialog box for creating a new Wi-Fi network. Enter the network name (SSID), and select WEP encryption if desired. If you select WEP encryption, then you will need to tap on WEP Key to set up the encryption keys.

To change the IP or DNS settings, bring up the Wi-Fi Setup application and select the network to edit. Press the Details button, then press Advanced in the next dialog box, and you will be able to choose between a static or dynamic IP address. You can also select whether to automatically choose a DNS server or to use specified primary and secondary DNS servers.

Smartphone

To start with, you may need to activate a Subscriber Identity Module (SIM) card in your smartphone (the provider who sold you your phone should have done this, but in some cases you will need to call the carrier to activate it). If you have a CDMA device (Verizon and Sprint), then you won't have a SIM card. Your phone (or SIM card) should have been activated when you signed up for wireless service. If not, you will need to contact your service provider to activate it. To support an Internet session, your wireless plan must be set up for data services. A few sample plans are listed in Table 6-1.

That's all you need to do to get set up. You should be able to access the Web [Hack #37] and check email [Hack #35].

Table 6-1. Sample wireless plans

Provider	Handset	With Tethering
Cingular	$24.99 MEdia Net Unlimited	$79.99 Data Connect Unlimited
Nextel	$19.99 Enhanced Data Service Plan	$54.99 Unlimited Wireless PC Access Plan
Orange UK	£88.13 (if you exceed 1000MB per month, you will probably get a nastygram)	(same as handset)
Sprint	$15 Unlimited Vision	None
T-Mobile	$4.99 Unlimited t-zones (email and web only)	$29.99 T-Mobile Internet
	$9.99 Unlimited t-zones Pro	($19.99 with a qualifying voice plan)
Verizon Wireless	$15.00 VCAST	$79.99 BroadbandAccess or NationalAccess Unlimited
	$4.99 Mobile Web (uses up plan minutes)	

Get Your Email on the Road

You are on the move and you don't have your desktop machine with you. Are you going to let that get in the way of your email fix? Of course not; you have your Palm device with you.

Once you have connected to the Internet [Hack #34], sending and receiving email is trivial if you are using a dedicated Internet service for your Palm device, such as a paired Bluetooth phone or cellular data service on a Treo.

Things get more interesting however, if you want more consistency between your desktop machine and your Palm device. Do you need to be able to search old emails? Do you want to sort email on the move and see those changes on your desktop? Will you be traveling to areas where you can't always get an Internet connection on your Palm device? There are two solutions: web-based email and IMAP.

Web-based Email

One solution is to use a web-based email service. The popular services such as Yahoo and Gmail have one limitation: you have to use one of their email addresses (@yahoo.com or @gmail.com). If you have an existing email account that you want to use, you can't use these services. Instead, you will need to use a web-based email aggregator. An email aggregator combines email from one or more POP accounts and presents it through a common web interface. You use a web browser [Hack #37] to access your email wherever you are. You will see the same interface, folders, and email from your desktop and Palm device. You can still use all of your existing accounts for reading and sending email. Any changes you make from your PDA will automatically be reflected on your desktop and vice versa. Also, if you end up somewhere where your Palm device can't connect to the Internet, then you may be able to find a local Internet connection (e.g., an Internet cafe) to continue working with your email until you regain Internet connectivity.

One useful email aggregator is Gopher King (*http://www.gopherking.com*). Gopher King (see Figure 6-13) provides access to all of your existing email accounts. You can also set up rules for processing your incoming email (move, delete, copy, etc).

An email aggregator is still a choice, but it may be more suitable to your lifestyle than either Yahoo or Gmail. These services each achieve a slightly different goal.

Figure 6-13. Reading email at GopherKing

IMAP

Another solution is to use IMAP instead of POP. IMAP is designed to support accessing an email account from multiple computers. So, you can read email and move messages into different folders on your desktop, and then pick up where you left off with your Palm device.

In addition to VersaMail, which is bundled with many Palms, there are many PalmOS email programs that support IMAP.

Agendus Mail. Agendus Mail (*http://www.iambic.com*) (see Figure 6-14) supports POP, IMAP, and SMS text messaging. You can send, receive, and manage emails and text messages. Agendus Mail allows you to manage multiple email accounts from your Palm device.

Aileron Mail. Aileron Mail (*http://www.corsoft.com*) (Figure 6-15) provides mail access via IMAP, POP, or SMTP. It also provides secure versions of IMAP and POP via SSL. It can also connect to a variety of different mail servers: Yahoo, MSN/Hotmail, AOL, Gmail, and Outlook Web Access.

SnapperMail. SnapperMail (*http://www.snappermail.com*), seen in Figure 6-16, also supports SSL for secure email. SnapperMail supports several popular mail services such as AOL, Gmail, and Yahoo.

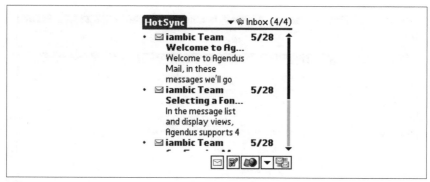

Figure 6-14. Agendus Mail inbox

Figure 6-15. Outbox in Aileron Mail

Figure 6-16. SnapperMail inbox

MailToGo. MailToGo (*http://www.webtogo.de*) provides POP, IMAP, SMTP, and ESMTP. ESMTP provides security enhancements over plain SMTP. MailToGo also provides support for sending and receiving email via a Bluetooth connection to a cell phone. MailToGo also handles SMS messages and can send faxes.

Chatter Email. Chatter Email (*http://www.chatteremail.com*) is a full-featured IMAP and POP client. It also has an innovative push feature that will send email to your Treo without having to manually download it. There is also a summary folder which contains a color-coded set of lines representing your other folders. You can see Chatter Email in Figure 6-17.

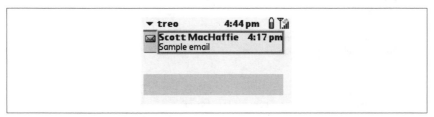

Figure 6-17. Inbox on Chatter Email

The web-based or IMAP solutions provide access to the same emails and folders from both your Palm device and your desktop. Each type of service has its own strengths and weakness. Be sure to pick a service that meets your needs.

HACK #36 Receive Alerts on the Go

How can you find out if your web server is down? You can set up your desktop to notify your Palm device when something happens.

You shouldn't have to manually check to see if your web site is up or not. Technology should be able to handle mundane chores like this. If you have a smartphone or wireless Palm device, then why not have it alert you when something goes wrong?

On your desktop machine, set up a simple script that checks to make sure your web site is alive. If the web site is down, then the script can send a text message (SMS) or an email [Hack #35] to your Palm device to let you know.

Test the following Python script out to make sure it works for you. Also, try running it with a non-existent URL to verify that the notification is working. Once the script is working, you can set up a cron job (Linux or Macintosh) or add it to Scheduled Tasks for Windows XP.

The Code

```
"""Check to see if a given web site is up or not.

Usage:
    python check_site.py <URL>
"""
```

```
import os, sys, urllib2, smtplib

# The following variables should be redefined to fit your system
_smtp_server = "outgoing.example.com"
# If you need to use SMTP AUTH, set this to 1.
# You will also need to set an SMTP user name and SMTP password
_authentication_required = 0
_user = ""
_password = ""
_to = "user@example.com"
_from = "webserver@mydomain.com"
_num_tries = 3

def is_site_up(url):
    """Checks to see if the given site is up"""

    try:
        urllib2.urlopen(url)
        return True
    except:
        return False

def check_site(url):
    """Checks several times to see if the given site is up."""
    count = 0
    up = False
    while not up and count < _num_tries:
        if is_site_up(url):
            up = True
        count += 1

    if not up:
        print "site %s not up." % ( url )

        # Construct a message
        mesg = "To: " + _to + "\n"
        # Note the extra blank line between Subject and body
        mesg += "Subject: Server down\n\n"
        mesg += "The web site: " + url + " is down.\n"

        # Send email notifcation using SMTP
        session = smtplib.SMTP(_smtp_server)
        if _authentication_required:
            session.login(_user, _password)
        result = session.sendmail(_from, _to, mesg)

        if result:
            print "Sent mail. Status = " + str(result)
    else:
        print "site %s is up." % (url,)

if __name__ == '__main__':
    if len(sys.argv) == 2:
```

```
        check_site(sys.argv[1])
    else:
        print __doc__
```

Running the Code

Save the code in a text file called *check_site.py*. Replace _smtp_server, _to, and
_from. If your server requires SMTP authentication, then set _authentication_
required, _user, and _password as well.

Invoke the script on the command line as follows:

% python check_site.py *url*

This will test the given URL to see if it is alive or not. If not, then the script
will send a message to the email you specified in _to. You might want to test
with a non-existent URL to make sure that you have the script configured
properly, then check with the URL you actually want to monitor. When the
script is working, then you can add it to Scheduled Tasks in Windows or set
up a cron job on Linux or Macintosh.

Hacking the Hack

You can send these emails as an SMS quite easily. Most wireless providers
have email addresses that automatically forward emails to a phone number
as SMS. Table 6-2 shows a partial list of US operators. Simply replace
<number> with the 10-digit phone number (no spaces or dashes, e.g.,
5035551212@messaging.nextel.com) when you send the email. Keep in mind
that a single SMS may contain at most 160 characters. Be aware that the
wireless providers may put a limit on the number of consecutive messages
that go through their email-to-SMS gateways to cut down on SMS spam.

Table 6-2. U.S. mobile operator SMS gateways

Operator	Email
Nextel	*<number>@messaging.nextel.com*
Sprint PCS	*<number>@messaging.sprintpcs.com*
AT&T Wireless	*<number>@mobile.att.net*
Cingular Wireless	*<number>@mobile.mycingular.com*
Verizon Wireless	*<number>@vtext.com*
T-Mobile	*<number>@tmomail.net*

Surf the Web On- and Offline

HACK #37

You can surf the Web even if your Palm device is not connected to the Web.

Surprisingly, you don't even need the ability to connect to the Internet to view the Web with your Palm device. If you want to look at arbitrary web sites, or you need to view live (up-to-date) pages, then you do need to be connected to the Internet [Hack #34]. In that case, you would use a standard web browser or an Internet suite.

However, Access (who recently acquired PalmSource) makes an excellent, full-featured browser called NetFront that is bundled with some devices. Web Browser Pro is available for some Tungsten and Zire models. For a comprehensive overview of the browsers available for Palms, see *http://www. palmsource.com/interests/browsers/*. However, many sites lend themselves well to offline reading. There are many web browsers available for the Palm and Treo. Some models include a web browser called Blazer.

Some sites are very useful only if you have a live Internet connection, but would not be very useful as static content. One such example is the extremely useful (at least if you live in Portland) *http://www.tripcheck.com*. This site is run by the Oregon Department of Transportation. It provides an average-speed map for the local Portland freeways, color-coded red, yellow, and green. You can use it to check which way you should go to avoid traffic.

For those of you who read web sites that aren't quite so dynamic, another solution exists. There are some offline web browsers available for Palm devices. An offline web browser comes with both a desktop component and a Palm component. The desktop component allows you to choose which sites or pages you want to read. You can also choose how many levels of links to follow, how much data you are willing to download for a single site, and how often to update your local copy of the site. You can also select whether or not to download images.

You can use iSilo (see Figure 6-18) as an offline web browser in addition to using it as a document reader [Hack #23]. There is a companion program called iSiloX which allows you to convert web documents to the internal iSilo format. The iSiloX program (Figure 6-19) can also set up the converted documents to be transferred on your next HotSync.

For example, you could set up the desktop component to grab Slashdot (*http://slashdot.org*), follow links one level (to get the text of the articles from the headlines), and to download at most 100K. Then, the desktop would update a local copy of Slashdot at whatever interval you requested. When you HotSync your Palm device, the latest copy that was downloaded from the Web will be transferred to your device.

Figure 6-18. iSilo viewing the iSilo home page

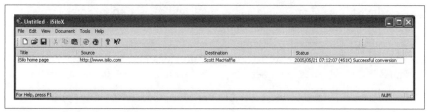

Figure 6-19. iSiloX document converter

Another great tool is plucker (*http://plkr.org*). Plucker is an open-source tool that allows you to convert web pages, e-books, and text documents for reading on a Palm device. There are desktop converters available for Windows, Linux, and Mac OS X.

You can download news or blog sites for ever-changing content, or you can download static pages for reference. You will need to update the amount of content you download and the frequency with which you perform a HotSync depending on how much time you spend reading offline content. If you are seriously addicted to reading blogs, then you probably want to get a dedicated RSS reader [Hack #38].

HACK #38 Read Syndicated Content

Have a favorite RSS feed? Wish you could read it on the move with your PDA? There are several RSS readers available for Palm devices.

On the desktop, RSS readers can take many forms. One of the simplest is the Live Bookmark capability in Firefox. This function creates a bookmark folder from an RSS feed. The folder contains one link for each item in the feed. You can see the name of the link but no description or metadata.

What Is RSS?

RSS is a technology for letting users know about new posts or articles on a web site. An RSS feed returns a list of articles (or posts or headlines) with descriptions and links.

The technology first became popular as a way of staying up-to-date with blogs. As it became more widely used for blogs, news sites adopted it. Now, you can find aggregators (such as Bloglines, *http://www.bloglines.com/*) that collect RSS feeds from multiple sites and even search engines that return results as RSS feeds.

The basic idea is simple. To produce an RSS feed, a web site produces a specially-formatted XML page. For each item (news headline, blog, post, or article), the XML page provides a name, a link and a description. Some forms of RSS can also include metadata such as author and date. RSS is standard—so standard that you get five different versions to choose from. Yay us. The two most common formats are RDF, which provides better metadata support, and RSS 2.0, which is a simpler format (but which also has the necessary support for podcasting).

More sophisticated RSS readers let you view one or more RSS feeds in the main window. The best readers let you read the descriptions and metadata without having to spawn new windows.

There are not as many choices on a Palm device as there are on a PC or Mac, but there is a little bit of variety.

mNews

The mNews RSS reader (*http://www.motionapps.com*) only works on Treo 600s and 650s. It provides controls for managing and grouping feeds, and you can read the feeds or the linked articles themselves. mNews can display embedded images, but it does not display dates, authors, or other metadata.

Quick News

Quick News (*http://standalone.com/palmos/quick-news/*), seen in Figure 6-20, can function as either an online or offline reader. It can display metadata such as dates and authors. It also allows searching and sorting by metadata. Quick News allows you to group feeds into categories, browse through feeds, and expand descriptions inline. You can also follow the links if you are connected to the Internet **[Hack #34]**.

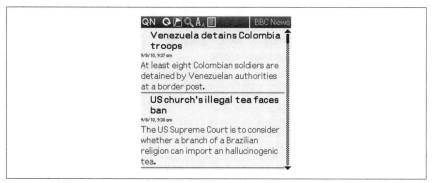

Figure 6-20. Quick News viewing a BBC News feed

Sunrise

Sunrise (*http://laurens.typepad.com/*), seen in Figure 6-21, is a Windows-based program which converts web sites and RSS feeds into documents for Plucker (*http://www.plkr.org/*). Plucker (see Figure 6-22) is a document reader for Palm OS devices.

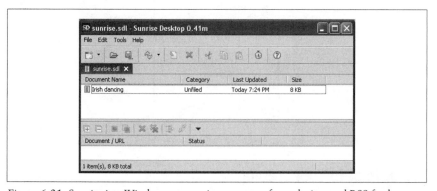

Figure 6-21. Sunrise is a Windows conversion program for web sites and RSS feeds

You have another choice for viewing RSS feeds. If you have a web browser on your Palm device [Hack #37], then you can use a web-based aggregator to view your feeds. Web aggregators take one or more feeds and group them for your convenience. One of the most popular aggregators is Bloglines (*http://www.bloglines.com*). Bloglines allows you to subscribe to multiple RSS feeds and view them all from a single interface. There is a mobile version at *http://www.bloglines.com/mobile*, which you can see in Figure 6-23.

All of these techniques allow you to stay up-to-date with your feeds. Even though you are on the move, you can still keep in touch with news and other information.

Figure 6-22. Plucker, an offline document reader

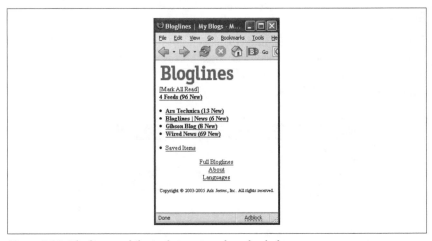

Figure 6-23. Bloglines mobile site being viewed on the desktop

HACK #39 Post to Your Weblog

Ever have that perfect thought for your blog but forgotten it before you got back to your computer? With your wireless-enabled PDA, you can post as fast as you can tap from wherever you are.

To start with, you will need to be connected to the Internet [Hack #34].

If your blog editing is entirely Web-based, then you can simply use your browser to add a new entry or edit an existing one. This procedure is no different than updating your blog from your PC.

Remote Access to Desktop Blogging Software

There is another solution if you use desktop software for editing your blog: use Virtual Network Computing (VNC, *http://www.realvnc.com*). With VNC, you can use your desktop blogging software [Hack #40] directly from your Palm device.

Palm-based Blogging Software

You can also run dedicated blogging software directly on your Palm device. These programs allow you to add or edit posts locally and update them on the Web. You need to have your hostname, login ID, and password to access your blog with these programs.

HBlogger

HBlogger (*http://www.normsoft.com/hblogger*) supports popular sites such as:

- LiveJournal (*http://www.livejournal.com*)
- Blogger (*http://www.blogger.com*)
- MovableType (*http://www.movabletype.org*)
- UJournal (*http://www.ujournal.org*)
- DeadJournal (*http://www.deadjournal.com*)
- Blunty (*http://www.blunty.com*)
- NeedlessPanic (*http://www.needlesspanic.com*)
- Plogs (*http://www.plogs.net*)
- Caleida (*http://www.caleida.com*)
- GreatestJournal (*http://www.greatestjournal.com*)
- TypePad (*http://www.typepad.com*)
- Weblogs (*http://www.weblogs.com*)

HBlogger can include images in posts. You can see the account selection screen in Figure 6-24.

mo:Blog

mo:Blog (*http://www.tektonica.com/projects/moblog*) supports several blog APIs: blogger, metaWeblog, and MovableType. With that support comes support for popular blogging sites like Blogger (*http://www.blogger.com*), MovableType (*http://www.movabletype.org*), and TypePad (*http://www. typepad.com*). mo:Blog can upload images as well. You can see an example of editing a post in Figure 6-25.

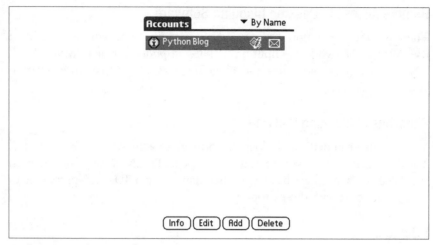

Figure 6-24. HBlogger account page

Figure 6-25. Editing a post in mo:Blog

Plogit

Plogit (*http://plogit.sourceforge.net*) is the only open-source program in this list. Using Plogit, you can tell at a glance which entries are local, online, or online but locally updated. In Figure 6-26, you can see a post that has been created locally and has not yet been uploaded to the server. You can also delete local or online entries. Plogit supports Blogger (*http://www.blogger. com*), MetaWeblog, and MovableType (*http://www.movabletype.org*). Plogit does not appear to support uploading images.

SplashBlog

SplashBlog (*http://www.splashblog.com*) allows you to easily publish a photo blog. Snap some pictures, add a caption, and then post them to your blog (Figure 6-27). The software includes a free online photoblog account.

Figure 6-26. Viewing posts in Plogit

Figure 6-27. Sample photo blog entry in SplashBlog

Vagablog

Vagablog (*http://www.bitsplitter.net/vagablog*) supports the Blogger API. It has been tested with Blogger (*http://www.blogger.com*), JournalSpace (*http://www.journalspace.com*), and MovableType (*http://www.movabletype.org*). You can see an example of Vagablog in use in Figure 6-28. Vagablog has been open-sourced, so it will probably be moving to SourceForge (*http://sourceforge.net*) soon.

Any of these solutions (web-based, remote access to your desktop, or Palm-based software) can help you keep your blog updated while on the move. The photo blog provides a different notion of a blog—very useful if your Palm device has a built-in camera.

```
┌──────────────────────────────────────────────┐
│        ▐▀▀▀▀▀▀▀▀▀▀▀▌                           │
│        ▐ Vagablog ▌                            │
│        ▐▄▄▄▄▄▄▄▄▄▄▄▌                           │
│        This is a test of the Vagablog          │
│        blogging software.                      │
│                                                │
│        One text editor looks much the same     │
│        as another.                             │
│                                                │
│        It seems functional, though.│           │
│                                                │
│                                                │
│                                                │
│                                                │
│        ( Post )                                │
└──────────────────────────────────────────────┘
```

Figure 6-28. Editing a post in Vagablog

HACK #40 Control Your Computer Remotely

Have you ever wanted to do something on your computer from across the room? How about from the other side of the world?

It can be useful to be able to access your desktop machine remotely. You could check server logs, restart failed services, or even post to your weblog [Hack #39]. If you have a home network, you can set up all of your computers so that they are accessible remotely.

VNC (Virtual Network Computing) is an open-source application that is designed to allow one machine to control another machine over a network. It was originally developed at Bell Labs. VNC is also useful for collaboration. Multiple viewers (clients) can connect to the same server. Each viewer has its own cursor. You can use these cursors to point to content on the remote machine. The viewers display the cursors for all of the other viewers as well. Each cursor is displayed differently from the others so you can tell them apart.

The server side comes in Windows, Mac, and Linux flavors. You can download these versions and get more information from the main VNC web site (*http://www.realvnc.com*). There are other versions of VNC available as well. For Windows and Linux machines, there is TightVNC (*http://www.tightvnc. com*). For Windows, there is also UltraVNC (*http://www.ultravnc.com*). UltraVNC supports server-side scaling. For Macs, you will need OSXvnc (*http://www.redstonesoftware.com/vnc.html*). The built-in VNC on Macs doesn't work with PalmVNC.

You will also need an application to access the server. In typical computer-speak, this application would be called the *client*, but VNC uses the term *viewer* instead. The Palm viewer is called PalmVNC (*http://palmvnc2.free.fr*). You can also download UltraVNC for Windows with PalmVNC.

For a different kind of remote control experience, check out the Pebbles Project (*http://www.pebbles.hcii.cmu.edu/*), which makes a variety of remote control products for Palm devices. For example, their SlideShow Commander is a specialized application for remotely controlling PowerPoint Presentations. If you're on a Mac, check out Salling Clicker (*http://homepage.mac.com/jonassalling/Shareware/Clicker/*), a general-purpose remote control package that can be extended with a little bit of AppleScript programming.

Set Up VNC on Your Desktop

To access your desktop remotely, you need to know its external IP address. If you have a single computer which is directly connected to the Internet and has a static IP address, that's easy. All you have to do is look up your IP address in the appropriate place and write it down for use in setting up PalmVNC.

If you have a dynamic IP address (e.g., your home computer is sitting behind a router), the situation is a little more complicated. You need to consider using an IP publishing service (see the "IP Addresses" sidebar). An IP publishing service will typically let you choose a hostname within their domain. You end up with a name like *hostname.domainname.com*. Keep this symbolic address handy for setting up PalmVNC.

Download and install the appropriate version of VNC on your desktop machine. After VNC has finished installing, run the configuration part of it. You will be able to choose a password for VNC, as you can see in Figure 6-29. Choose a good password (at least eight characters and a mixture of upper- and lower-case characters, numbers, and punctuation). This password is all that is needed to access your machine over the Internet, so choose carefully. Either write it down or remember it—you will need the password when configuring PalmVNC.

Setting up OSXvnc on a Mac. When you run OSXvnc, you will see a screen similar to Figure 6-30. Select a display number (usually 1) and port (usually 5901). Set a password—this is the password which you will use when you log in from PalmVNC.

When your Mac is set up, then you can proceed to setting up PalmVNC (explained later in this hack). When everything is working and you are connected, you should see a screen on your Palm device that looks like Figure 6-31.

IP Addresses

All computers on the Internet have an Internet Protocol (IP) address. An IP address uniquely identifies any computer on the Internet. It is used for routing sessions to the appropriate machines.

An IP address is a four-part number. Each part is a number in the range 0-255. The numbers are separated by decimal points. Thus, an IP address can look like 192.168.0.1 (a typical home network address) or 127.0.0.1 (a reference to the local machine). IP addresses can be static, which means that the addresses don't change. Internet Service Providers (ISPs) usually charge a bit more for static addresses. Most people (at least at home) have dynamic addresses. A dynamic address is assigned by the ISP on a periodic basis. Thus, a dynamic address won't necessarily be the same from day to day. To connect to a computer over the Internet, you either need to know its IP address, or you need to have a name for it (e.g., *www.google.com*). The name is then mapped via a Domain Name System (DNS) server into the actual IP address.

If you have a dynamic IP address, you can hook up with a free service to publish the address. The service acts as a DNS server for a name you select (a hostname within their top-level domain) and maps that name to your computer's current dynamic IP address. You download a small program that runs on your PC which updates the IP address for your computer in the service's DNS. You get to choose a hostname for your computer within the domain names offered by your service. Then you can refer to your computer via *hostname.domainname.com*. Some service providers are No-IP.com (*http:// www.no-ip.com*), Dynu (*http://www.dynu.com*), and DynDNS.org (*http:// www.dyndns.org*).

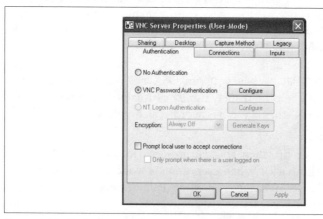

Figure 6-29. VNC server configuration under Windows

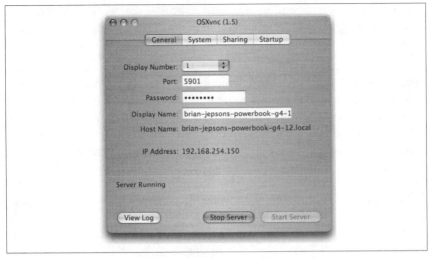

Figure 6-30. OSXvnc general setup screen

Figure 6-31. Viewing a Mac desktop with PalmVNC

Securing the connection. You will need to open some ports in your firewall for VNC. VNC itself needs access to ports 5900-5902. By default, VNC sends information (including passwords) as plaintext. You can use ssh (a secure protocol that can encapsulate other types of connections such as VNC; see *http://www.openssh.org* for more information) instead for more security. You will need to open port 22 in your firewall for ssh, if you have not already done so.

Some of the servers (notably TightVNC) have ssh setup by default. For other VNC servers, the process is fairly simple. From the client side of a desktop machine, you want to run something similar to the following:

```
ssh -L 5902:localhost:5901 remotehost -l username
```

PalmVNC comes with a plug-in that does RSA-40 encryption. If you want more security than that, you can tunnel your VNC connection through a VPN.

Whenever VNC is running, it will look for incoming connections. If you have a personal firewall (Norton Internet Security, ZoneAlarm, or others), you will need to set the firewall to allow VNC to access the Internet. If you have a port-based firewall, you will need to allow access to the ports that VNC uses. By default, VNC uses ports 5900 and 5800 (port 5800 is only used for a Java-based viewer), but you can change those ports if you want to under the Connections tab.

Setting up VPN. There is a Palm VPN client called Mergic VPN (*http://www. mergic.com*). To set up a VPN, you need to have an externally visible IP address for your desktop machine. Enter that IP address into Mergic VPN in the area titled VPN Server Name or Address, as shown in Figure 6-32. You can create multiple VPN accounts for connecting to different machines. Set the account name in the Account edit box. Note that this name is only used to distinguish between different setups in Mergic. The actual username for logging into VNC goes into the User Name field. You can also choose to have Mergic VPN autoconnect to the server when specific applications are run.

Figure 6-32. Setting up Mergic VPN

You can run PalmVNC using the VPN from Mergic. You can see Mergic VPN being set to run automatically whenever PalmVNC runs in Figure 6-33.

You also need to configure a VPN service on your desktop machine.

Setting up VPN on Windows XP. Windows XP comes with VPN available by default. Start by creating a new network connection (from the Network Connections section of the Control Panel). Select an Advanced Connection,

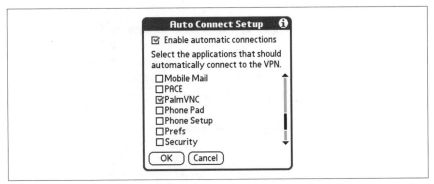

Figure 6-33. Setting up MergicVPN to autoconnect whenever PalmVNC is run

as you can see in Figure 6-34. The next dialog box lets you select the advanced connection options. *Select Accept incoming connections*, as you can see in Figure 6-35. Next, choose the device that you want to allow VPN connections from. Then, you will need to allow VPN connections in the following dialog box, shown in Figure 6-36. After that, select the users that you want to allow to use VPN. You will need one of these usernames (and the corresponding password) when you set up Mergic VPN. The final steps are to allow access to different types of services (at a minimum you need TCP/IP—others are your choice) and to set up the IP address for your computer.

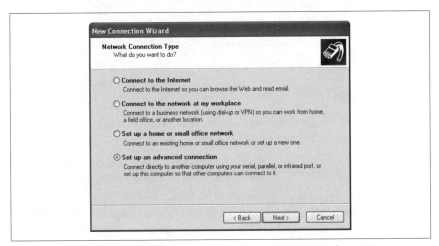

Figure 6-34. Selecting an advanced connection to set up VPN in Windows XP

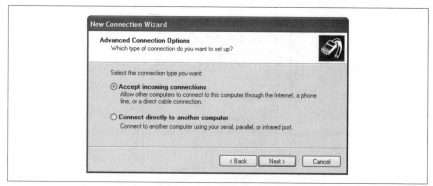

Figure 6-35. Selecting Accept incoming connections from the Advanced Connection Options dialog box

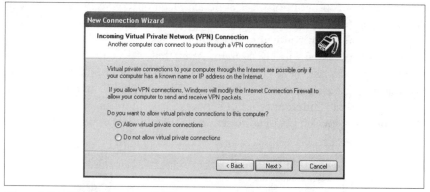

Figure 6-36. Allowing incoming VPN connections in Windows XP

Set Up PalmVNC

Download PalmVNC from *http://palmvnc2.free.fr*. Unzip it and install *palmvnc.prc* onto your Palm device.

Connect your Palm device to the Internet [Hack #34] and run PalmVNC. Set up a new connection to your desktop machine, as you can see in Figure 6-37. Enter the IP address for your desktop machine and the password you used when setting up the VNC server, and then tap OK and Connect from the next form. If everything is working, you should now see your desktop on your Palm device.

You can move around the desktop by using the narrow scrollbars on the right and bottom of the screen. If you set up server-side scaling when you were configuring the server, then you can select from PalmVNC's menus (or the Advanced dialog box, as seen in Figure 6-38) to take advantage of scaling. At 1:2 scaling, you can view a 640×640 desktop on a 320×320 Palm device or even up to a 640×960 desktop on a 320×480 Palm device. That's large enough to see (and do) a decent amount.

```
        ■ Connection Properties  ❶
    Connection Name:
    My currentServer

    Server name or IP Address:
    host.company.com

    Display Number:  0
    (usually 0 for a Windows server,
    1 for a Unix server)

    Server Password:  -Prompt-
    ( OK ) (Cancel)    (Advanced...)
```

Figure 6-37. Setting up a PalmVNC connection

```
        ■ Advanced Properties  ❶

    Begin at:  X: 0      ,Y: 0
       Scale:  1: 1

    NT user name:  username
    NT password:   -Prompt-

    Base port:  5900
      ☑ Enable desktop sharing

      ( OK )  (Cancel)
```

Figure 6-38. Advanced connection properties in PalmVNC

No matter which operating system your desktop is running, you can still control it with PalmVNC and an appropriate server. Make sure that you use an appropriate level of security for the environment you are in (running over a local network or running over the Internet).

HACK #41 Control Your Home Theater

You know that stack of infrared (IR) remotes that's always spilling onto the floor? Your Palm can take the place of all of them.

You need software to convert your Palm into an infrared (IR) remote. Two choices are OmniRemote (*http://www.pacificneotek.com*) and NoviiRemote (*http://www.novii.tv*). You should look at the home theater devices that these two programs support and pick the one that is compatible with your gear.

If neither program covers all of your devices, then you have a couple of choices. If you have the remotes for your devices, and you are looking at simplifying down to just your PDA, then you can switch the applications into learning mode. Line up the remote and your Palm device on a flat surface with the IR end of the remote pointed at the IR port on your PDA and run through all of the important buttons on the remote. Save the buttons for each device under a unique name.

If you are missing some of the remotes, then you can try to find an IR code library on the Web. One good source is RemoteCentral (*http://www. remotecentral.com*), which has IR files under the Files tab on the home page. The files for the Philips Pronto can be used with OmniRemote by using a converter from the OmniRemote web site. If you can't find your specific device, then try to find a similar device by the same manufacturer.

Once you have all the codes for the devices you want to control, it is time to create button layouts. There are a variety of interesting button layouts on the Web. The web sites for the IR software have some button layouts, as does RemoteCentral. You can look at these for inspiration.

You should keep in mind what you want to do with each button layout that you create. For example, a common layout is *watching DVDs*. To do this, you may need to turn on the TV, DVD, and home theater systems. You could combine these actions into a macro, then have a single Power button that turns everything on. Then, you might also need: volume, play, pause, stop, fast forward, rewind, menu, and arrow keys. A button layout for watching TV might include a number pad, channel-up, and channel-down buttons.

Hardware

One of the big problems with using a Palm as an IR remote is the limited range of the Palm's IR port.

Fortunately both companies also provide hardware versions of their products. OmniRemote sells a Springboard module for the Handspring Visor and Handspring Prism. You will need to find a used Visor **[Hack #50]**. The Visors have a Springboard slot in the top that can take plug-in modules. All you have to do is stick the OmniRemote module into the Visor. The software is pre-loaded on the module.

NoviiRemote makes a product called the NoviiRemote Blaster. This is an SD card that functions similarly to the OmniRemote product, except that it works with SD-compatible devices such as recent Palm-branded devices.

At the time of this writing, I was unable to locate a similar product for the Sony Clié.

Detailed Instructions

The first part of these instructions applies to using both OmniRemote and NoviiRemote.

1. Make sure that the software (or hardware) that you want to use is compatible with your PDA. If not, consider buying a cheap Palm to use as a dedicated remote control.

2. Even if you plan on buying a hardware device to install in your PDA, start by downloading the corresponding trial software—you need the software to check that it can control your device.

Using NoviiRemote. NoviiRemote provides standard button layouts for a number of different devices, such as TVs, VCRs, etc. You can easily switch between different devices, as you can see in Figure 6-39. Here are some tips for using NoviiRemote:

Figure 6-39. NoviiRemote

- Use the trial version of NoviiRemote to make sure that the controls work. Start with the default *codebases* (collections of remote control codes) that came with the software. For each device you want to control, try out the included codes to see if the functions you want to use work.

- If the included codebases don't work, then check the company's web site for additional (or user-supplied) codebases. Download these and try again.

- If the downloaded codebases don't work, then you can try using OmniRemote instead, if it supports your PDA.

- If none of that works and you have the remote controls for the devices which don't have codebases, then you can put the program into "learn" mode and teach it all of the buttons. If you are successful with this, then you can help other users by uploading the results back to the company's web site.

Using OmniRemote. OmniRemote (Figure 6-40) provides macros in addition to the standard buttons. A macro can combine multiple actions (e.g., turn on the TV and turn on the VCR). OmniRemote supports a different set of devices natively than NoviiRemote. Here are some tips for getting the most out of OmniRemote:

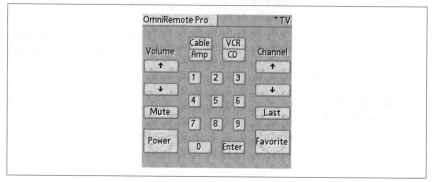

Figure 6-40. OmniRemote Pro

- Use the trial version of OmniRemote to make sure that it can control your devices. You need to either program all of the buttons yourself (if you have the corresponding remote controls), or you can try to find codes on the Web.

- If you want to find codes on the Web, start by downloading *CCFCnvt. zip* from the OmniRemote web site, unzipping it, and installing it. This program converts remote control libraries from *.CCF* format to the internal format that OmniRemote uses.

- Go to RemoteCentral (*http://www.remotecentral.com*) and look under Files for code databases for the Philips Pronto device, a popular remote that can control just about anything. These databases are the *.CCF* files that you can convert. If you find files that seem to match your home theater devices, then download them. You will need to unzip the files as well.

- Run *CCFCnvt.exe*. You will see a screen similar to Figure 6-41. In this program, you will hit Read CCF to load each of the CCF files that you downloaded in the previous step. For each file, look for the device that you want (many of the CCFs are for a set of devices so you may need to experiment to figure out which file corresponds to the device you want).

When you find the appropriate device in CCF Converter:

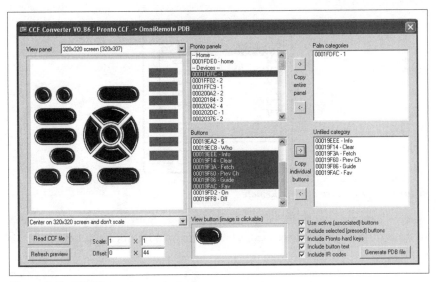

Figure 6-41. CCF Converter

1. Use the arrow button to add it to your selected list. Repeat this for each device.

2. When you have collected all of your devices, then select Create PDB File to generate a new database with your devices in it.

3. Go to your Palm Desktop and press Install or Quick Install.

4. Click Add and choose the PDB file that you created in the previous step.

5. HotSync your PDA to download the configurations.

6. Test to make sure that you can correctly control your devices now.

 One of the nice features of OmniRemote is that you can create macros. For example, you might have a *Watch DVD* macro that turns on the TV, DVD, stereo, or home theater, and sets the volume to the correct level for a DVD. To create a macro, start by creating a new button and select Macro as the type of button. Then click on the Edit Macro button and hit Insert. You will be prompted to tap buttons to add them to the macro.

Either of these devices can simplify your remote controls. You will end up with a single Palm device instead of a stack of remotes. You also have the ability to create sophisticated macros to handle multiple common chores at once. You can see an example of creating a macro to turn on the TV, increase the volume, and switch to channel 25 in Figure 6-42.

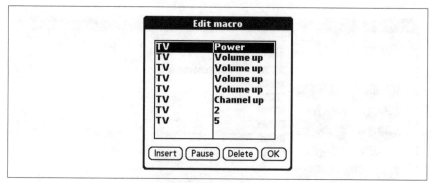

Figure 6-42. TV macro in OmniRemote

Macros can give you a lot of power in a single button. With a few macro buttons on a single page, you can easily perform a number of functions.

## CHAPTER SEVEN

System
Hacks 42–49

System hacks are more technical than the hacks in the other chapters because they cover details that are closer to the operating system itself. Thus, they are hacks for writing your own programs and playing with the launcher. These hacks are good starting points for exploring the Palm operating system. From here, you can branch out and discover your own hacks.

With a limited number of hacks, much is left for you to find on your own. For example, some of the built-in applications have Easter eggs in them. If you search around on the Web, you can find information on them.

As you play with these hacks, think about the reasoning that went into them. You can take the fundamental ideas and apply them to other parts of the Palm OS or to other applications. The essence of hacking is finding a clever way of doing something that you want to do, not necessarily following a recipe out of a book.

HACK #42 Simulate a Palm

Are you looking at acquiring multiple Palm devices? If so, it is useful to know which Palm OS versions will work with the applications you want to run. It is straightforward to test applications against a range of Palm OS versions.

If you don't have access to Palm devices with a range of Palm OS versions, then there is another solution. The Palm OS Developer Suite (*http://www. palmos.com/dev/tools/dev_suite.html*) contains the Palm Emulator and the Palm Simulator. The emulator and simulator are two separate tools that do basically the same thing, but they handle different versions of Palm OS. Between them, these tools cover Palm OS versions from 3.0 to 6.0 and let you test Palm applications on your PC.

The emulator (Figure 7-1) and simulator (Figure 7-2) use ROM images to do their magic. You will select a ROM image the first time you run either program. Look for one that has "EN" in the name—something like *PalmOS412_FullRel_EZ_enUS.rom*. The "EN" means that it is an English-language version of the ROM. You should pick a release ROM image because a *release* image will be the most similar to an actual device. You can also set the amount of memory (RAM) available to the device, and you can set the screen resolution. Thus, you can try various combinations to see what works.

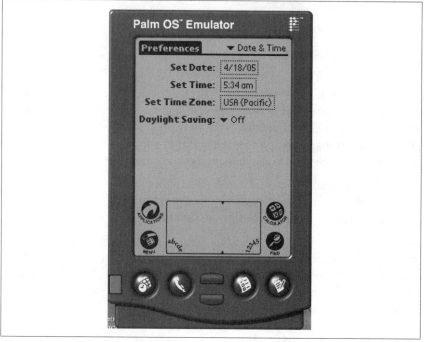

Figure 7-1. Palm Emulator, v4.x

To get started, follow these steps:

1. Download the Palm OS Developer Suite from *http://www.palmos.com/ dev/tools/dev_suite.html* and install it.

2. Find the emulator under *C:\Program Files\PalmSource\Palm OS Developer Suite\PalmOSTools\Palm OS Emulator\Emulator.exe* and create a short-cut to it on the desktop or add it to the Programs menu.

3. Do the same for the Palm OS 5 Simulator at *C:\Program Files\PalmSource\ Palm OS Developer Suite\sdk-5r4\tools\Palm_OS_54_Simulator\release\ PalmSim_54_rel.exe* and the Palm OS 6 Simulator at *C:\Program Files\ PalmSource\Palm OS Developer Suite\sdk-6\tools\Simulator\6.0.1\Release\ PalmSim.exe*. Note that the specific paths may vary depending on what versions of Palm OS are included in the developer suite you download.

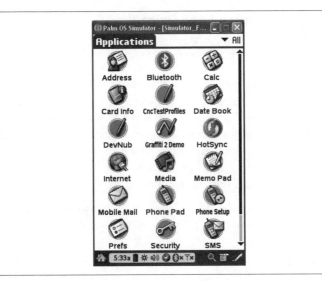

Figure 7-2. Palm Simulator, v6.x

4. Download the Palm applications you want to test. Unzip them if necessary. If an application comes with a custom installer, then run the installer. After the installer completes, the files will be in a folder similar to *C:\Program Files\Palm Handheld\<HotSync ID>\Install*. A typical Palm application consists of one or more PRC files and one or more PDB files.

To test against Palm OS 3.0 – 4.x, run the emulator. To test against Palm OS 5 or 6, run the corresponding simulator. You may need to download additional ROM images for specific OS versions. You can find those at the same site where you got the developer suite.

When the emulator or simulator is running, you can right-click on the screen and use the Install → Database menu item to install the PRC and PDB files for the applications you want to test. You can also just drag-and-drop applications from a Windows folder into the emulator to install them. Hit the Home silk-screen button and launch the applications that you are testing to see if they work.

Between the simulator and emulator, you can test Palm OS versions from 3.x through 6.x. Programs may work on a real Palm device that don't work on the emulator or simulator. It depends on the nature of the program. Basic applications should work the same on different platforms, but anything that pushes the hardware (e.g., barcode scanning or beaming) may not work on the emulator or simulator.

Make Upgrades Less Painful

#43 Upgrading your PC or switching to a new Palm is fairly easy, but there are some things you need to keep in mind when you migrate your data.

Before you migrate to a new PC or Palm, make sure you've got everything synced up. On your current Palm, you need to check all of your applications to make sure that all the data you want to save is set to synchronize. The built-in applications automatically sync all of their data, but some third-party applications allow you to select which data to sync. For example, ShadowPlan lets you select whether or not to sync for each list, and Balance-Log [Hack #12] lets you select how long to keep data.

After you have checked the sync preferences, go ahead and do a HotSync to bring both your Palm device and your PC up to date.

New Palm Device

If you are switching to a new Palm device, then make sure it has been fully charged. Run through the basic setup—date, time, time zone, digitizer, and HotSync name. Use the same HotSync name that you used for your old device. Many applications use a registration scheme which is tied to the HotSync username—even changing the capitalization of the name can cause these applications to think they aren't registered.

Install the desktop software that came with your Palm device. This will insure that your Palm device and your desktop are current with each other. Install the new desktop software into the same location as your old desktop software. If you are upgrading to a Treo, then you may be given an option when installing the desktop software to remove known incompatible applications. If you are planning on installing all of your existing third-party applications at once, then you should turn this option on. If you are going to install the third-party applications one at a time (or not reinstall them at all), then this option doesn't matter.

If you want to install all of your existing third-party applications, go ahead and perform a HotSync to bring over your data. You may need to reinstall some of your applications manually, especially applications that had their own installers. You may also have to remove some applications—sometimes old applications that you deleted will reappear when you sync to a new Palm device.

If you don't want to automatically reinstall your existing third-party applications, then you need to rename the *C:\Program Files\Palm Handheld* *<HotSync ID>\Backup* folder to something else, like *Backup.old*, before doing a HotSync with your new device.

When you have all of your applications installed, do one last HotSync to bring over the data from any applications that you had to manually install. Check to make sure that your data was successfully transferred to your new Palm device. If anything didn't make it, you might find it easier to beam the missing items from your old device to the new.

If your Palm device is crashing after upgrading, then the cause is likely third-party applications. To fix the problem, you need to do a hard reset (to clear memory) and install your third-party applications one at a time until you figure out which one is causing the problems. Rename the folder *C:\Program Files\Palm Handheld\<HotSync ID>\Backup,* which stores third-party applications. Rename it to something else and then install programs one at a time from there. When you find the application that crashes, delete it from your Palm device and from the *C:\Program Files\Palm Handheld\<HotSync ID>\ Backup* folder. Whenever you install an application, it is automatically copied to the Backup folder. You may also want to do another hard reset on your Palm device to clear out any accumulated junk.

Performing a Hard Reset

To perform a hard reset, you need to locate the reset button on your Palm device. This is usually on the back of the device. Look for a hole in the case with the word Reset next to it. You will need something to poke the reset button with—look at your stylus. If you are using the standard stylus that came with your device, then there are a couple of options. The stylus itself may fit inside the hole. If not, then see if either end of the stylus unscrews. If so, then you may be able to use that to press the reset button.

Pressing the reset button by itself performs a soft reset. In a soft reset, the Palm device is restarted, but your data and programs are left alone.

A hard reset will remove all of the programs and data on your Palm device, leaving you with just the built-in applications (and no data for them). To perform a hard reset, hold the power button down while pressing the reset button. Hold the power button down until the Palm Computing screen appears. You will be given a chance to confirm that you really want to remove all of your data.

Another choice is to use a new username for your new Palm device. Copy over the built-in data by exporting the data from the Palm desktop software and then importing the data under your new username. Then, install just the third-party applications that you want to use on your new device. The only problem with this approach is that any applications you've purchased that are registered under your original HotSync name won't be registered anymore.

New PC

After you HotSync to your old PC, you are ready to get set up on the new PC. Install the desktop software on your new PC, and then do a HotSync. If any of the third-party applications on your Palm device have *conduits*, then you will need to install the desktop components on your new PC. Applications that came with their own installers (as opposed to *.prc* and *.pdb* files) likely have conduits. You will need to copy the installers to the new PC and run them. You need to HotSync again to run the conduits. If the applications have desktop versions, then you can check the desktop versions to make sure the data was transferred.

> Conduits are programs that run on your PC to transfer data between your PC and your Palm device. Conduits sometimes just transfer existing Palm databases, but conduits can also be written to convert between desktop and Palm formats. For example, many document readers for PDAs come with conduits that convert popular desktop formats (e.g., Microsoft Word format).

You may want to copy a couple of folders from your old PC to your new one. Your old PC will have a folder similar to *C:\Program Files\Palm Handheld*. (*Palm* might be replaced with *Sony* or the manufacturer of your PDA.) Under that folder will be another folder named from your HotSync name. There are two useful folders under there, *Backup* and *Archive*. These folders contain data and applications that have been installed on your PDA. You can copy these folders to your new PC so that you can easily install older applications if you need to.

New PDA Step by Step

Here are the detailed instructions for upgrading to a new Palm device, so follow along:

1. Check sync preferences for third-party applications on your old PDA.

2. HotSync your old PDA.

3. Fully charge your new PDA (or install batteries).

4. Run through basic PDA set up (date, time, HotSync name).

5. Install new desktop software into the same location as the existing software. If you are bringing over all the third-party applications at once, then you can set the option to ignore known incompatible applications.

6. If you are going to bring over third-party applications one at a time, rename the *C:\Program Files\Palm Handheld\<HotSync ID>\Backup folder* to something else.

7. HotSync your new PDA to bring over data and some applications.

8. Check to see if any applications did not get installed—if so, install them using custom installers (if the programs came with custom installers) or using the Palm desktop Install button.

9. Perform a HotSync to bring over the new applications.

10. Perform a HotSync again to bring over any data for the new applications.

11. Remove any applications that were installed that you no longer need.

12. Check that all of your data was transferred to the new PDA—if not, beam the missing data over from your old PDA.

13. Change the username on your old Palm device to avoid confusion or accidental corruption of your data.

New PC Step by Step

Here are the detailed instructions for upgrading to a new PC. If you are doing both at the same time, start by upgrading the Palm device first, then your PC.

1. Check sync preferences for third-party applications on PDA.

2. Perform a HotSync to your old PC.

3. Install Palm desktop software on your new PC.

4. Perform a HotSync to new PC.

5. Copy custom installers and third-party desktop applications to your new PC.

6. Run custom installers on your new PC to set up conduits.

7. Perform a HotSync again to run conduits.

8. Check desktop applications to see if data was transferred from the Palm device.

9. Look for *C:\Program Files\Palm Handheld* (or *<Manufacturer> Handheld*) on your old PC. Under that folder will be a folder named for your HotSync name. Copy the *Backup* and *Archive* folders from there to the corresponding location on your new PC.

These steps should help remove problems caused by upgrading. Generally, upgrading is fairly painless, but once in a while you run into a problematic third-party program that should be removed or upgraded.

HACK #44 Reprogram the Hardware Application Buttons

Do you use some applications much more often than the built-in applications? Assign a hardware button to them for easy launching.

The simplest way to reprogram the hardware buttons is to use the built-in Preferences application. Launch the Preferences application, and then select Buttons from the category list. From there, you will be able to change which application each of the hardware buttons launches, as you can see in Figure 7-3. You may also be able to change which application the silk-screened calculator button launches. This can be useful if you have replaced the standard calculator [Hack #15]. On a Treo, you can set two applications for each button. One application comes up when the button is pressed by itself. The other comes up when you press the Option key in addition to the application button.

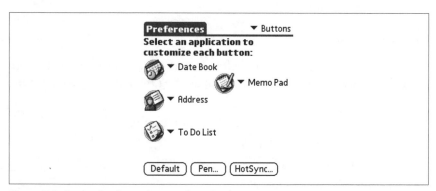

Figure 7-3. Setting hardware buttons from Preferences

This works well if you want to permanently replace the applications that the buttons launch. However, if you want to have the ability to launch more than four applications (e.g., for roleplaying [Hack #18]), then you will need to install a third-party program such as ButtonLauncher or TealLaunch.

ButtonLauncher

ButtonLauncher (see Figure 7-4) allows you to map up to nine applications per hardware button. You can find it at *http://palmsource.palmgear.com/ index.cfm?fuseaction=software.showsoftware&prodid=41233#*.

Figure 7-4. Using ButtonLauncher to set hardware buttons

TealLaunch

TealLaunch (see Figure 7-5) allows you to invoke applications through combinations of button presses and pen strokes. You can find it at *http://www. tealpoint.com.*

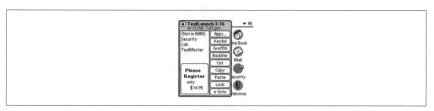

Figure 7-5. TealLaunch configuration screen

You can also use the launcher to make it easier to get to applications. You can either set up categories or replace the launcher [Hack #45].

Improve the Launcher
You can tweak the built-in launcher a bit. However, the built-in application launcher lacks some features found in various third-party launchers.

The launcher provides some useful options. You can find related hacks for reprogramming the hardware buttons [Hack #44] and changing launcher options [Hack #46].

See More Applications

The standard launcher displays applications using Icon view. This view displays the largest icon available for each application. While this looks nice, it also reduces the number of applications that you can see at once. To fix this, you can switch to List view.

1. Switch to the launcher.

2. Choose the Preferences item under the Options menu.

3. There will be an option to control how you view applications. Set it to List to see more applications. You may also have choices like Icon (small) or List (small). These choices (if available) will also display more applications. You can see the preferences dialog box in Figure 7-6.

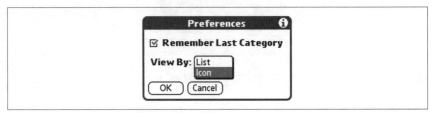

Figure 7-6. Launcher Preferences dialog box

Easy Hotkeys

You can set up shortcuts with any launcher. Create a special category called *Favorites* (or something like that). Move the applications that you use most often into that category. The key to getting the most out of this hack is to make sure that the applications all fit on one screen. That way, the applications are only a single button press and a tap away. You should also set your launcher to remember the last category [Hack #46], if that option is available. Most launchers do that automatically.

Choose a Better Launcher

Typical features of replacement launchers include:

- File operations on internal memory cards
- Multiple categories and individual preferences for each category
- Customized backgrounds and icons
- Additional options for launching applications from the hardware buttons
- File management
- Detailed system and file information

There are several popular launchers.

ZLauncher. ZLauncher (*http://www.zztechs.com*), seen in Figure 7-7, has good support for expansion cards. You can move programs or databases to an internal memory card, and you can even launch applications from a memory card.

Figure 7-7. ZLauncher

MegaLauncher. In addition to supporting application launching, Mega-Launcher (*http://www.megasoft2000.com*), seen in Figure 7-8, also has an excellent file manager.

Figure 7-8. MegaLauncher

FacerLauncher. FacerLauncher (*http://www.pocketcraft.com*) also has the ability to display a summary of your day, as you can see in Figure 7-9. The basic summary includes any appointments for the day, but it can also be customized with plug-ins for various applications. There are plug-ins for weather, bank balances, and more.

Some devices have their own launchers. The Sony Clié and Tapwave's Zodiac both have unique launchers. Their launchers are designed to take advantage of hardware-specific controls—the JogDial on the Clié and the gaming buttons on the Zodiac.

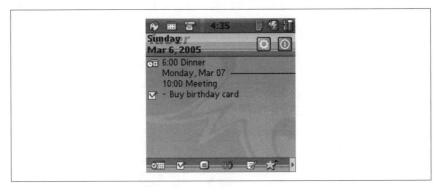

Figure 7-9. FacerLauncher showing Today view

 Tweak Every Setting

#46 Scattered throughout the system and in the built-in applications are some options you can set to make your Palm device easier to use.

The built-in applications are so handy as-is that we rarely realize that there are useful settings buried inside them. Tips for specific built-in applications can be found in other hacks. As well, you can find specific tips on the launcher [Hack #45]. Another set of useful information is on improving your text entry [Hack #24].

Launcher

You can view more applications [Hack #45] in the launcher.

Sony Clié Standard Launcher

The Sony Clié's standard launcher provides options for remembering the last category and the last application. The last category setting puts you back in the last category you were viewing when you switch back to the launcher. The last application is related to the Jog Navigation style. One setting for Jog Navigation is Popup. In the Popup mode, rotating the jog dial brings up a list of the applications in the current category. If *Remember last application* is turned on, then the last application you launched will be highlighted in the menu.

Clié Launcher View Settings

The Clié has its own unique launcher, as you can see in Figure 7-10. In addition to the standard icon and small icon options, the Clié launcher also provides options to view applications stored on memory cards, display an animation when launching applications, use drag-and-drop for working with applications, and control whether beaming only works for sending data.

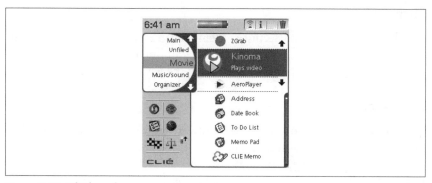

Figure 7-10. Clié launcher

Date Book

The Date Book provides options under several different menu items. You can change the font size with the Font... menu item. Note that making the font larger will decrease the number of visible time slots in the Daily view. However, decreasing the font size from the default value does not increase the number of visible time slots. The Preferences... menu item lets you select the start and end times for the calendar's Daily view, as well as letting you set alarm preferences. Display options lets you tweak both the Daily view and the Monthly view. There are also privacy settings for password-protecting (hiding) your appointments.

Address Book

The Font item is the same as it is for the Date Book, except that making the font smaller does increase the number of visible items. Preferences allows the program to remember the last category and toggle between listing first and last name versus company and last name. Rename Custom Fields is nice—you can set the custom field names to be birthday, anniversary, or any other common information that you want to enter. And of course, there is the ever-present Security option to prevent unauthorized users from seeing your contacts.

To Do

To Do doesn't have a lot of options—just Font and Security.

MemoPad

In addition to Font and Security, MemoPad has an option under Preferences to switch between alphabetic sorting and manual ordering. For manual ordering, you can tap-and-drag items in the list view to reorder them.

Preferences

This application lets you map the hardware buttons to different applications and set formats for times, dates, and numbers. You can control sound
and the auto-shutdown. You can also add shortcuts, which are abbrevia-
tions that will automatically be expanded when you write them.

Treo Preferences

The Treo has some unique preferences, accessible via the Preferences application. You can set the date and time to be read from the cellular network.
Under Date and Time, select *Enable local network time* if available.

Because the Treo is a cell phone, it has several phone-like preferences, as
you can see in Figure 7-11. You can set whether or not the phone vibrates.
The default setting is that the Treo will vibrate when the ringer is turned off,
and it won't vibrate when the ringer is on.

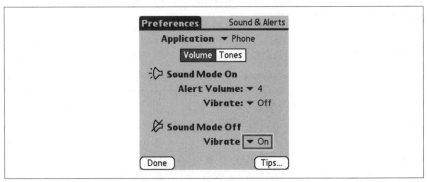

Figure 7-11. Treo sound and alert preferences

You can set a Keyguard feature to help prevent random items bouncing
around and activating your Treo while it's in your pocket or purse. The Keyguard feature lets you use the center button to unlock the phone when you
turn it on. The Keyguard preferences lets you control when (or if) this feature gets activated—never, immediately, or after a delay. You can also disable the touchscreen while you are on a call, which prevents you from
accidentally hanging up or dialing numbers with your face while you are on
a call.

Extend Your Palm

HackMaster isn't just the name of an RPG, but is a collection of system extensions (hacks) for your Palm device.

HackMaster (and its later replacements) manages third-party extensions (hacks) to the Palm OS. Over time, some of the more popular hacks have been incorporated into the operating system itself. For example, new Palm devices support tapping in the title area of an application to bring up the menu. Older Palm devices didn't support this, so someone wrote Menu-Hack. MenuHack provided this functionality before it was available in the OS itself.

Other hacks include superFindHack [Hack #7] for improving the built-in Find and various hacks related to entering text, such as CapsHack and MidCaps-Hack.

There are some limitations to hacks and HackMaster, however. Starting with Palm OS v5.0, HackMaster no longer works. Hacks and HackMaster itself have been so popular that they have spawned several other extension managers or replacement tool sets, such as Teal Master (*http://www. tealpoint.com*) and pToolSet (*http://www.paulcomputing.com*).

> To find out what version of Palm OS you are running, go to the launcher and select Info from the Application menu. From the Info form, tap the Version button and you will see the Palm OS version number at the top of the form.

An extension manager handles extensions (hacks) that conform to a common interface. The most common interface for Palm OS extensions is the HackMaster interface. Extension managers allow you to install, delete, enable, and disable hacks. Some extension managers provide additional features.

HackMaster

HackMaster (*http://www.daggerware.com*), seen in Figure 7-12, was the original extension manager. HackMaster defined the interface that subsequent hacks and extension managers have followed. HackMaster works well on Palm devices through Palm OS 4.x. However, PalmSource chose to disable hacks in Palm OS v5.0.

How Do Extensions Work?

Motorola 68K chips provide for custom opcodes (instructions used by the microprocessor). Any opcode of the form $Axxx (hexadecimal) is a custom opcode. Some versions of the 68K chips also have custom opcodes in the $Fxxx range.

These opcodes are frequently used for system calls in operating systems—early Macs, Atari STs, and Palm OS versions through 4.x all made use of these opcodes. The opcodes trigger custom (operating system-specific) handlers. An extension patches into this process.

The proper way for an extension (in general, not specific to HackMaster) to patch one of these opcodes is to store the address of the existing handler when the extension is first installed and to restore the previous handler if the extension is removed. Also, the extension should call the original handler as well, after it has finished handling the event. Thus, you can build up a chain of extensions which all patch the same opcode. Extension A can call Extension B which calls Extension C which calls the original function.

There is a problem with this approach, though. What happens if Extension B is removed? How does Extension A get notified to point to C instead of B? The HackMaster extension API addresses this. Conforming extensions can be added and deleted in any order, and the links will be properly updated.

When the Palm OS switched to the ARM processors, these opcodes were not available. Thus, they decided to drop support for HackMaster-style extensions. Palm OS 5.0 and later do support a limited form of extensions. New-style extensions can register to receive notification on certain system events.

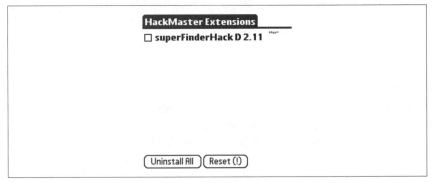

Figure 7-12. HackMaster

X-Master

X-Master (*http://linkesoft.com*) is a free replacement for HackMaster. In addition to the standard enable and disable functions, X-Master allows you to see which functions each hack patches, as you can see in Figure 7-13. In some cases, this may allow you to find conflicts or resolve strange behavior. To find this information, select a hack from X-Master and press the Details button. X-Master also supports having sets of hacks and easily switching between them. You can also get information on all applications (not just hacks) that are patching system functions.

Figure 7-13. X-Master showing Details view

TealMaster

TealMaster (*http://www.tealpoint.com*), seen in Figure 7-14, is a HackMaster replacement that emulates some hacks under Palm OS 5.0. When you run TealMaster under Palm OS 5.0, hacks are listed with icons indicating whether or not they are likely to run under Palm OS 5. Some known compatible hacks are TealMagnify (zooms in to make the screen easier to read), TealGlance (gives a Today view on powering on your Palm device—displays date, time, today's appointments, To Do items), and TealEcho (lets you see what you write in the Graffiti area). TealMaster supports sets of hacks so you can easily switch between different system configurations. The set support is sophisticated—you can configure TealMaster to switch sets when you change applications. TealMaster also allows you to configure the order in which hacks are invoked when more than one hack patches the same system trap.

pToolSet

pToolSet (*http://www.paulcomputing.com*) is not a direct HackMaster replacement. Instead of managing HackMaster extensions, pToolSet provides a set of its own tools (see Figure 7-15) which work on Palm OS versions 3.0-5.x. These tools do not patch the system traps, so they work despite the changes in Palm OS 5. pToolSet provides some of the same sorts of tools that are available as hacks. pToolSet includes a tool for improving

Figure 7-14. TealMaster

access to checkboxes and other controls, a tool for creating Date Book, MemoPad, and To Do items without leaving the current application, an info tool, a launcher tool, and several text tools.

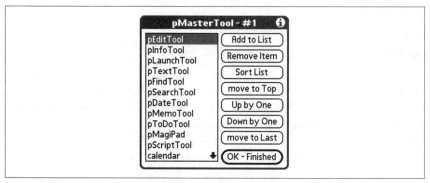

Figure 7-15. pToolSet listing some of the tools

There are also standalone tools and utilities of various sorts, such as battery and uptime meters. You can search for other tools at the various Palm software sites.

HACK #48   Investigate Your Palm's Databases

Every *.pdb* file on your Palm is a database associated with an application. Find out what databases are installed on your Palm device and get more information about them.

The simplest way to investigate *.pdb* files is to hit the Info menu item on the Applications menu in the built-in launcher. This will list the applications and some (but not necessarily all) of the *.pdb* files on your device. For example, if you have a document reader installed, then individual documents usually show up as installed *.pdbs*. From the Info menu, you have three display options: version, size, and records. For *.pdbs*, the version is frequently v0.0. This can help you distinguish a *.pdb* from an application.

Size is just how much memory the application or *.pdb* is using. Records indicates how many separate entries are in each *.pdb* or application. What a record contains is up to the person who wrote the program. It could be a single name, address, and phone combination, or it could be a single saved game.

You can use this level of investigation to try to find orphaned data. Sometimes, when you remove an application, one or more *.pdbs* may be left behind. For example, if you downloaded a Bingo game but later removed it, then you might find something like *BingoData*. In that case, you could delete it from the launcher.

Sometimes it can be unclear what some of the things in the list are. There are a number of run-time libraries that some applications use. These can have names like *CASL* or *WABA*. The problem with these items is that more than one program might be using them, so it is hard to tell if you can safely delete them or not. Usually, the side effect of deleting one of these is that if you run an application that requires the deleted library, it will crash. Then you have to reset your PDA.

There is a much more sophisticated tool that you can use to investigate *.pdbs* called PDBBrowser (*http://www.freewarepalm.com/utilities/pdbbrowser. shtml*). It allows you to View, Beam, Delete, or Create new databases. After you select a database (Figure 7-16), then you can view it. Viewing a database lets you see all the records one at a time. You can delete or edit individual records and create new records within a database. Note however that many records are in a binary format rather than a text format. This means that you may not be able to interpret them in PDBBrowser.

Figure 7-16. Selecting a database in PDBBrowser

If the database's records are stored as text, then you can even edit them by hand. This isn't as easy as using the original program, but you might be able to fix a corrupted database. Also, you can delete records that look corrupted—but make a copy of the database first, so you can restore it if need be.

HACK #49   Write Your Own Programs

Writing programs for your Palm is not as hard as you might think. You can write programs on the desktop and download them to your Palm device. You can also write small programs directly on your Palm device itself.

There are many different development environments for Palm OS devices. You can get Integrated Development Environments (IDEs) for your desktop machine which let you build programs to download to your Palm device. You can also get some interesting applications that let you develop programs (or scripts) directly on your Palm device. Of the development environments covered in this hack, the Palm OS Developer Suite, NS Basic, and Pocket Smalltalk are desktop environments. DragonForth and Pippy both run directly on a Palm device. Even if your development environment runs on a Palm, you can still write your programs at your desktop by running the Palm OS Emulator or Simulator. You can find additional development environments. Two good resources are the Palm OS developer site (*http://www. palmsource.com*) and an independent page that covers lots of resources at *http://www.winikoff.net/palm/dev.html*.

Palm OS Developer Suite

The newest development environment for Palm OS 5 and Palm OS 6 is Eclipse. The good news is that Eclipse is open source. The bad new is that Palm's customized version of Eclipse only runs on Windows XP. Eclipse itself is cross-platform, but the extensions for Palm development only run under Windows. Eclipse is an Integrated Development Environment (IDE) that supports various languages and platforms through plug-ins. A custom version of Eclipse is available from PalmSource called the Palm OS Developer Suite (*http://www.palmos.com/dev/tools/dev_suite.html*), which you can see in Figure 7-17. The first step in developing applications from the desktop is to download and install the developer suite (you'll need to register for a free account at that web site before you can download the suite). This will set you up for programming in C or C++.

Mac, Linux, and Unix users aren't left out in the cold, however. See *http://www.palmos.com/dev/tools/gcc/* for information on PRC-Tools, a GCC-based development toolchain for non-Windows platforms.

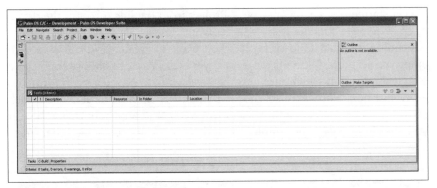

Figure 7-17. Palm OS Developer Suite, no project open

The Palm Developer Suite supports several ways you can work with projects. It can fully manage the project, handling all of the dependencies and *makefiles*. The developer suite can also manage projects which use an external makefile.

A *makefile* is a file containing a collection of directives, dependencies, and commands. It is used by your development environment to compile your project from source code into its final form (an executable). In the simplest of all possible programs, where you have one source file and one executable, a makefile is not strictly necessary. However, real-world programs are often made up of several source files and in some cases, multiple projects (for example, if you are a game developer, you may have one project containing all the *library code* that is shared between all your games and a separate project for each game). In such cases, a makefile is essential. For more information on makefiles, and the program (make) that drives them, see *Managing Projects with GNU make*, Third Edition (O'Reilly, 2004).

The Palm operating system itself comes in two versions. Up through Palm OS 4.x, Palm devices ran on Motorola's 68K series of chips. With Palm OS 5.0, the 68K chips were replaced with an ARM processor. Palm OS 5 and 6 devices can run 68K programs in a special compatibility mode. Programs written specifically for the ARM processor will be much faster than those written for the 68K, however. When you create a new project, you will need to choose between a 68K application and an ARM application. If you want to support the widest range of Palm OS versions (e.g., Palm OS 4 or previous versions), then choose 68K. If you need the fastest possible application (and are willing to live with the Palm OS 5 or later restriction), choose ARM.

To get started quickly, choose New Project from the File menu in the developer suite. This menu item will let you choose an appropriate wizard depending on what kind of project you want to create. You can create an empty project and fill in all the details yourself. You can choose to create a simple application which provides the basic code to create a main form and an About box. You can also choose to create a simple puzzle game which provides a game screen, an instructions screen, and an About dialog box. If you choose to create the simple game, then you will get a screen that looks like Figure 7-18.

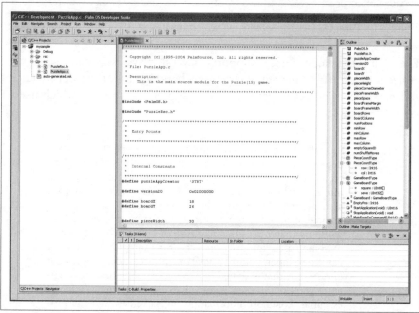

Figure 7-18. Sample project in the Palm OS Developer Suite

For now, choose the simple application. Step through the remaining steps to finish creating your first project. When the project has been created, then you can build and run it. Select Rebuild All from the Project menu. This will compile the program and create a *.prc* file. The compilation messages will appear in a pane in the lower part of the main window.

If the compilation completed successfully, then you are ready to run the application. It is better to test the application on the desktop before downloading it to your Palm device. Select Run... from the Run menu. This brings up a dialog box that lets you select a simulator to run on, as you can see in Figure 7-19. Select between a Palm OS 5 simulator [Hack #42] and a Palm OS 6 simulator. You can also choose between debug and release versions. The debug versions have all of the standard controls set to different background colors. The debug version also detects a number of errors, which can be helpful in tracking down problems in your code. The release version tries to recover from errors silently, behaving more like a real PDA.

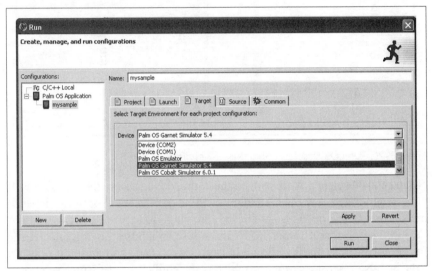

Figure 7-19. Dialog for running an application from the developer suite

After you have chosen an appropriate simulator, you can run your application. You should be able to select it from the launcher, and you should be able to bring up the About box. Congratulations, you have just written your first Palm OS application.

Once you have gone through the basic process of building and launching a sample application you can start tweaking it to do something useful. The Palm Developer Suite has a list of the files in a pane on the left side of the main window. Click on the files to bring them into the main workspace. From there, you can edit the files to put in interesting behavior.

One file deserves special mention. The resource file (.rsc) contains all of the user interface controls—forms, buttons, edit controls, and so forth. Double-click on the resource file to bring up the resource editor (see Figure 7-20) which lets you graphically edit the resources.

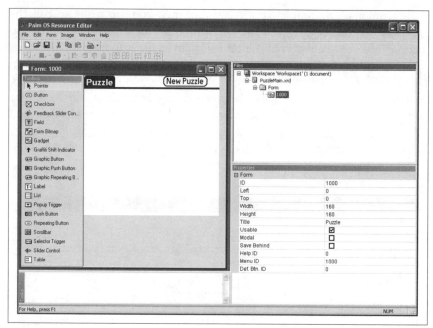

Figure 7-20. Palm OS Developer Suite Resource Editor

Testing and debugging. You can connect the debugger to the simulator. If your program hits any bugs, then you will be given a set of options, depending on the nature of the bug. The options include Ignore, Reset, Quit, and Debug. For non-fatal errors, you can choose to ignore the bug and let the program continue running. Sometimes this works and sometimes it doesn't. You can also reset the simulator which is the equivalent of doing a reset on a Palm device. You can quit the simulator or enter the debugger. Entering the debugger lets you use the Palm OS Developer Suite to view your program's source, set breakpoints, and inspect variables.

A useful technique for testing Palm applications is called *Gremlins*. A Gremlin is a random event. PalmSource recommends testing any Palm application for at least one million Gremlins before releasing it to the public. You set up Gremlins by right-clicking on the Palm Emulator and selecting the Gremlins menu item. You can choose to run one or more series of gremlins, as you can see in Figure 7-21. If you run more than one series at a time, then you get to choose how often to switch between the different series. You also get to choose how many events to generate and which applications to run.

Further information. The developer suite provides online help for the Palm API for both Palm OS 5 and Palm OS 6. It also provides a general programming guide for the Palm operating system that discusses the Palm OS

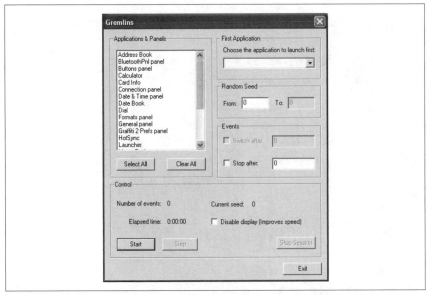

Figure 7-21. Gremlins panel for testing in the emulator

philosophy. The PalmSource web site (*http://www.palmsource.com*) has a knowledge base with articles, answers to questions, links to tools, and information on known bugs.

There are several good books which cover Palm OS programming. The most comprehensive book is *The Palm OS Programming Bible,* Second Edition by Lonnon Foster (Wiley 2002). Another interesting book is *Palm OS Game Programming* by Nicholas Pleis (Premier Press 2001).

Distributing your software. If you write a program that you think might be of interest to other people, then you can look at different ways of distributing it. If you want to make it open source or distribute it for free, you can put it up on your own web site. Open source projects can also be put up on SourceForge (*http://sourceforge.net*). You can also put programs of any flavor (free, open source, or commercial) on the main Palm software sites like PalmGear (*http://www.palmgear.com*), Handago (*http://www.handago.com*), and PalmSource's directory (*http://www.palmsource.com*). You can also try to get links from the Open Directory (*http://www.dmoz.org*).

NS Basic

If you are more comfortable programming in Basic, then you could look at NS Basic (*http://www.nsbasic.com/palm/*). This is a desktop development environment for building programs which you can download to your Palm device. You can see a sample project in Figure 7-22.

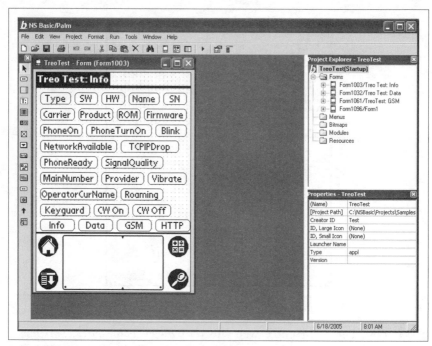

Figure 7-22. NS Basic development environment

NS Basic seems a lot like a version of Visual Basic for Palm OS. There is a visual form designer for creating resources. You can double-click on an item in the form designer to add an event handler. NS Basic requires a runtime library on the Palm device. NS Basic only runs on Windows. NS Basic comes with the Palm OS Emulator and integrates nicely with it. You can launch the emulator from within the IDE and transfer your programs (and the runtime libraries) directly to the emulator or set up your program to be transferred to your Palm device at the next HotSync.

Pocket Smalltalk

Explore Smalltalk on your Palm device with Pocket Smalltalk (*http://www.pocketsmalltalk.com*). This is an open-source IDE for developing Smalltalk programs that run on your Palm device. You can see a sample project in Figure 7-23.

The latest version of Pocket Smalltalk only runs on Windows. Pocket Smalltalk itself is written in Smalltalk. There are two versions of Pocket Smalltalk, each of which uses a different underlying version of Smalltalk. The latest version of the IDE uses Dolphin Smalltalk, which only has a Windows version. There is an older version of the IDE available which runs

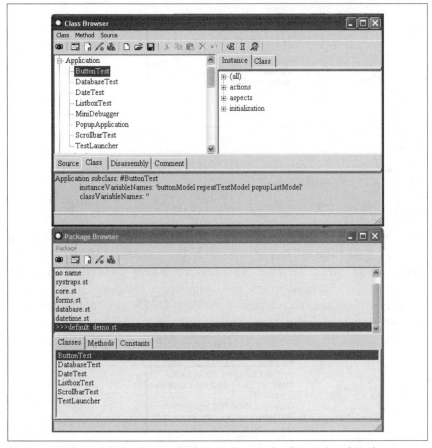

Figure 7-23. Part of the Pocket Smalltalk IDE showing the class and package browsers

under the Squeak version of Smalltalk. Squeak has been ported to many platforms including Windows, Linux, and Mac.

DragonForth

If you want to play with Forth, DragonForth (*http://sourceforge.net/projects/dragonforth/*) is an implementation which runs on your Palm device, as you can see in Figure 7-24. You can build your own programs without needing to use your desktop environment.

Forth is an interesting language. It is stack based and works using Reverse Polish Notation, like most HP calculators. That means that operands (2 and 2 in the example) go on the stack first, and that the operators come at the end. Operators take the last items that were added to the stack and return their results to the stack.

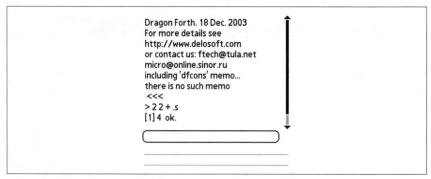

Figure 7-24. DragonForth console

Pippy

Pippy (*http://pippy.sourceforge.net*) is an open-source implementation of Python 1.5 for Palm OS (see Figure 7-25). There are some limitations—not everything in Python has been ported to try to keep the size down. Pippy was built and compiled under the Metrowerks compiler. If the project becomes active again, then a port to the Palm OS Developer Suite might be in order.

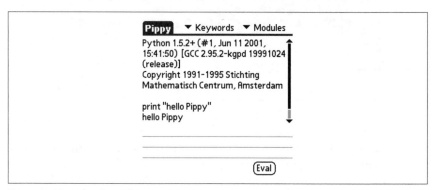

Figure 7-25. A simple Python expression in Pippy

I think that Python is a nice language for someone learning to program. The syntax is fairly simple, but there is a lot of power as well. There are some excellent tutorials on Python—check out the main Python web site (*http://www.python.org*) for more information.

There are a couple of tips to make writing Python programs in Pippy easier.

All multi-line Python scripts, whether entered directly into Pippy or imported from a memo, must be terminated with a blank line (i.e., the cursor needs to be on a line by itself, following the last statement). Otherwise, you will get a syntax error on the last line of your script.

You can write scripts in MemoPad and import them into Pippy. Create a category named Python in MemoPad. The first line of each script needs to be something like *#module.py*. Run Pippy and execute the following commands:

```
import memoimp
memoimp.install()
import module
```

Then you should be able to use the module you wrote. To make life easier, you can create shortcuts **[Hack #24]**. Useful shortcuts include *memoimp*, *memoimp.install( )*, and the names of any modules that you are working on.

Another tip is to use single quotes instead of double quotes for strings. It is easy to confuse two single quotes in a row for a double quote—this can lead to hard-to-find bugs.

## CHAPTER EIGHT

Hardware
Hacks 50–55

A Palm device is useful by itself, but depending on your needs, you may want to extend its capabilities with additional hardware. Hardware can make a Palm device better at things it is not naturally good at—entering text, using GPS, and other such applications.

Most Palm devices have now standardized on SD cards, but you can also find Bluetooth accessories. For older devices, you may be able to find accessories on the Web. Hardware hacks on Palm devices have a long tradition going back to some of the earliest Palm devices. These hacks cover a range of devices from the Palm III up through the latest Palm devices. The Handspring Visor was designed to support hardware hacking with the Springboard slot. Schematics and details on how to build modules were readily available from Handspring.

Some of these hacks are more low-level, while others are more about extending the Palm's capabilities.

HACK #50 Find Cheap Palms

So you've come up with a cunning plan—the laser sharks are ready and all you need are a couple dozen Palms to run your battle robots, all without breaking your evil overlord bank account.

The first step in finding cheap Palm devices is to figure out what your requirements are. Do you need color devices or will black and white suffice? How much RAM do the devices need? Are there any special requirements like a headphone jack, camera, or wireless connectivity? Finally, figure out what OS version you need. Check the applications you want to run and see what versions they work on. If you're not sure, you can test software against a particular Palm OS version [Hack #42]. Find the range of versions that all of your applications work with.

---

eBay

The classic place to find anything for sale is eBay (*http://www.ebay.com*), of course. Palm devices can be found under a few different categories: Consumer Electronics/PDAs and Handheld PCs/Handheld Units, Cell Phones/Phones Only (Treos), and Consumer Electronics/GPS Devices (Garmin iQue). You can also search for devices by name (e.g., Clié, Visor, Palm, Zire, Tungsten) or by manufacturer (Sony, Palm, Handspring, Handera, Tapwave, Garmin) or by searching for Palm OS. You can sometimes find good deals by searching for typos such as "Plam" or "Zrie."

Amazon Auctions

Amazon (*http://www.amazon.com*) has auctions similar to eBay. Palm devices can be found under Computers and Software/Hardware/Handhelds/Palm, Electronics and Photography/Communications/Mobile Phones. Also, if you visit the product page for a particular device, Amazon will point out any used items that are available for sale.

Freecycle

Freecycle (*http://www.freecycle.org*) is an attempt to keep junk out of landfills. It can be very hit-or-miss, but you might be able to find some Palm devices. You sign up with a local Freecycle group. Then, if someone has something to get rid of, they can send an email to the group. Items in Freecycle are always free, but the chance of finding the specific item you want is low, so be flexible.

Government Surplus

You can occasionally find Palm devices through government surplus. These usually go fairly inexpensively even for newer models.

Computer Swap Meets

You might think that they are archaic in the Internet world, but there are still computer swap meets. Sometimes you might be able to find a set of Palm devices, especially if you aren't concerned about getting all the same model.

Electronics Stores

With Sony (at least in the United States) and Tapwave exiting the PDA market and the high turnover in models, you can sometimes find recent models at much less than their original prices. Also, electronics stores will sometimes carry refurbished (i.e., used) models at a significant discount. Fry's Electronics (*http://www.frys.com*) sometimes has great deals like this. You'll find *open box items* in electronics stores. These are discounted items that have either been returned or opened for some random reason. Be sure to ask whether the full warranty applies when you buy an open box item.

Non-Profit

If you are working on a non-profit project, then you might be able to get a donation from a Palm-device manufacturer. You would need to contact the manufacturer directly and explain the situation to see if they could help.

Palm PluggedIn Developer Program

If you are going to develop software for Palm devices, then you can join developer programs sponsored by the manufacturers. For example, Palm has a developer program called PluggedIn (*http://pluggedin.palm.com/*) that provides discounts on hardware for development purposes.

Patience is the key to finding cheap Palm devices. If you need something in short order, you may end up having to pay full price. If you have more time before you need the devices, though, you may be able to find a good deal.

HACK #51 Find a Better Stylus

The stylus is the most important accessory for your Palm device. It is important to choose the right one.

Choosing between a metal and plastic stylus is not a hack. If you are looking for a simple replacement stylus, this is not the right place to look. A hacker's stylus is multi-functional. It is a PDA stylus, but it is also a flashlight, multi-tool, voice recorder, or laser-powered death ray.

Many of these styluses can be found at different locations. The web sites listed here are not the only sources for them—your local electronics store may have many of the more common ones.

Laser Pointer

The Laser Pointer (*http://www.thinkgeek.com*; search for stylus) is a combination laser pointer, stylus, and ballpoint pen.

Cross MicroPen

The Cross MicroPen (*http://www.stylisource.com*) is a true replacement stylus that fits in the stylus slot in most Palm devices. It combines a stylus with a ballpoint pen.

Lighted Stylus

The PDA Light Stylus (*http://www.stylisource.com*) has a small LED in the tip so that you can use the stylus in the dark.

Comfort Stylus

The Comfort Stylus (*http://www.stylisource.com*) can wrap around your finger so that your finger itself becomes the stylus, as you can see in Figure 8-1.

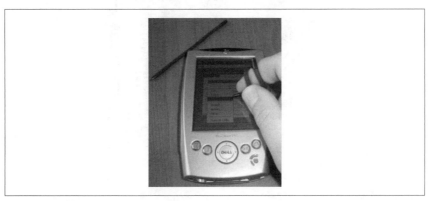

Figure 8-1. Comfort Stylus, twisted and straight

Voice Recorder

The Voice Recorder (*http://www.styluscentral.com*) is a combination stylus and 45-second voice recorder. This is an alternative to recording voice memos on your Palm device [Hack #26].

acura Stylus Tool

The acura Stylus Tool (*http://www.styluscentral.com*) is a true multifunction stylus. The stylus includes a small knife blade and scissors.

Infiniter XP Stylus Duo

The Infiniter XP Stylus Duo (*http://www.styluscentral.com*) combines a pen, stylus, laser pointer, and LED torch.

Swiss Army Pen/Stylus

The Swiss Army Pen/Stylus (*http://www.styluscentral.com*), seen in Figure 8-2, combines multiple tools into one, as you would expect from the name. This tool combines a stylus, Fisher Space Pen cartridge, scissors, small knife blade, file, screwdriver, and LED minilight.

Figure 8-2. Swiss Army Pen

S+ Nitespot

The Nitespot (*http://www.stylusplus.com*) is an illuminated stylus. Instead of having an illuminated tip like most other choices, however, the Nitespot has an illuminated body.

There are other styluses available, but these are some of the more interesting ones. New products come out constantly—you can check the referenced web sites to see what's current. Other good sites for reviews include Brighthand (*http://www.brighthand.com*) and The Gadgeteer (*http://www. the-gadgeteer.com*).

Find the Perfect Keyboard

Entering significant amounts of text with the stylus is a pain—that's why external keyboards were invented.

As usual, what kind of keyboard you should get depends on what your needs are. Do you need a full-size (laptop-style) keyboard? Do you want a mini-keyboard for portability and space?

Stowaway Keyboard

The Stowaway Keyboard (*http://www.thinkoutside.com*) comes in three models: infrared, Bluetooth (Figure 8-3), and a direct connect version (Figure 8-4). These keyboards are similar in feel to a laptop. You do need a stable place to rest the keyboard while using it—your lap won't be sufficiently stable.

Figure 8-3. Stowaway Bluetooth keyboard being folded

Happy Hacking Cradle

If you have a Palm III series device or are willing to pick one up [Hack #50], then you might be able to locate a Happy Hacking Cradle by searching the Web. The Happy Hacking Cradle is a cradle for a Palm III series device that lets you use any PS/2 keyboard.

Micro Datapad

The Micro Datapad (*http://www.mic-innovations.com*) is a mini-keyboard for the Palm m100 and related models. The keyboard is only slightly wider than a PDA. It plugs into the bottom of an m100.

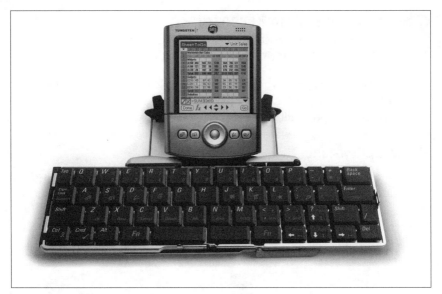

Figure 8-4. Tungsten connected to Stowaway direct-connect keyboard

Twiddler

The Twiddler (*http://www.handykey.com*) is a one-handed chording keyboard. A chording keyboard is one in which multiple keys are pressed simultaneously to enter a character. The Twiddler has a strap that fits over your hand, and then you use the fingers of that hand to hit the keys. The original Twiddler worked with the Palm devices through the use of a Hackmaster [Hack #47] extension called twiddleHack. It is unclear whether the current Twiddler 2 still works with Palm devices or not.

Any of these keyboards will make it easier to enter text and more practical to edit large documents on a Palm device. The Twiddler requires practice to become proficient.

HACK #53 Must-Have Accessories

Palms are powerful out of the box, but for specialized uses you might want to look at adding hardware.

If you want to expand your Palm device's capabilities, you are not limited to just memory cards. You can choose from SD cards and other types of accessories that go beyond simple memory. In addition to the items listed here, you can find add-on infrared transmitters [Hack #41] and keyboards [Hack #52].

Wi-Fi Card

Palm (*http://www.palm.com*) sells SD Wi-Fi cards. These cards provide 802.11b access on your Palm device. You can use these cards to connect to the Internet [Hack #34].

SD Backup Card

In addition to HotSyncing, you can buy an SD Backup card from Palm (*http://www.palm.com*). This card can back up the contents of your Palm device, which is useful if your data gets wiped out or if you need to do a hard reset. It is especially worthwhile for traveling. If you don't have your PC with you, how else would you restore your data? If you have an existing SD card that you would like to use to hold your data, then you should look at backup-buddyVFS (*http://www.bluenomad.com/bbvfs/prod_bbvfs_details.html*). You can use this program to back up critical data and programs to your memory card.

UniMount

The UniMount (*http://www.revolvedesign.com*) is designed to attach your Palm device to your car's dashboard. The UniMount allows you to see and work with your Palm one-handed. But please don't play Tetris while driving.

CardScan

Do you receive a lot of business cards? If so, then you might want to consider CardScan (*http://www.cardscan.com*). CardScan is a scanner designed exclusively for business cards. The scanned business cards can be imported into the Palm desktop's address book and then HotSync'd to your Palm device. Unless you get overwhelmed with business cards, however, it is simpler to just type them in.

Presenter-to-go

Presenter-to-go (*http://www.margi.com*) is a neat device. This is an SD card for your Palm device that allows you to display to a projector. It also provides support for displaying PowerPoint presentations.

Kirrio Navigation Pack

The Kirrio Navigation Pack provides a GPS attachment for your Palm device, together with software and U. S. maps. As a combination, this set can help prevent you from getting lost. It is available through retailers such as Amazon. Maps are also available for the United Kingdom and Europe.

GPS Navigation Kit

The GPS Navigation Kit from Palm (*http://www.palm.com*) is a navigation solution for your car. It provides a GPS module, software, and maps of the United States and Canada.

Hardware add-ons can fundamentally change what you can do with your Palm device. A GPS kit can help you navigate—hard to do with a bare Palm. A keyboard [Hack #52] can allow you to enter and edit large documents. Imagine trying to do that with a stylus.

Repair Worn Contacts

#54 If you sync too much, you can wear out the contacts on your Palm device. This hack shows how to repair these contacts.

If you sync your Palm device via a cradle or USB cable, then it is possible to sync too much. The mechanical connections on your PDA can be worn away by repeatedly connecting and disconnecting from the cradle or cable.

If you sync your PDA wirelessly, this won't be a problem unless your sync connection is also used for charging.

Even if you have a wired connection, you should be fine unless you sync every day for several years. You don't need to sync that frequently, unless you are either updating data on your Palm device that often or you are getting daily downloads of information (such as web sites, music, or video).

If you do sync enough that you wear off the contacts, there may be something you can do. Note that opening up your Palm will probably void your warranty, but by the time this happens, your warranty will have most likely expired anyway.

The first step is to get access to the connectors. On some devices, such as the Handspring Visor, this is trivial because the connectors are easily accessible without removing the cover, as you can see in Figure 8-5.

On other devices you will have to remove the cover, as shown in Figure 8-6.

Figure 8-5. Comparing access to connectors

Figure 8-6. Removing the cover

This may require a special screwdriver (such as a mini Phillips or a Torx T5), again depending on which device you have. Specialty screwdrivers can usually be found at electronics stores. With the cover removed, you should see something like Figure 8-7.

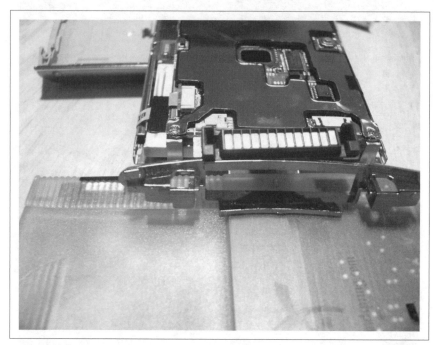

Figure 8-7. Cover removed

Once you have access to the connectors, you need to inspect them for signs of wear, as you can see in Figure 8-8. If there are obvious signs of wear or holes in the connectors, then you might be able to fix them.

There are pens you can buy at your local electronics store that draw out conductive lines (e.g., the Circuit Writer Pen). Take one of these pens and fill in any worn spots on the connectors, as shown in Figure 8-9. Be careful using these pens because they contain lead and a solvent. Work in a well-ventilated area and clean up carefully afterwards.

When the conductive mixture has dried, reassemble your device and try syncing it. If everything worked, you should be able to sync. If not, maybe it's time for a replacement Palm [Hack #50].

Figure 8-8. Signs of wear on the contacts

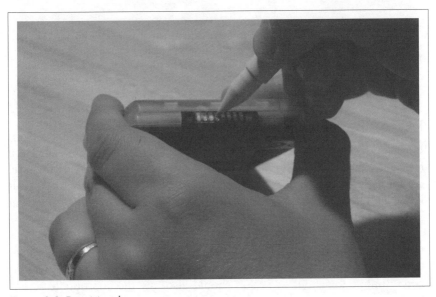

Figure 8-9. Repairing the contacts

Replace Your Batteries

#55   The rechargeable batteries in Palm devices don't wear out very often. If they do wear out, you can change them yourself.

There are two types of rechargeable batteries in different Palm models. Newer Palm devices have a big rechargeable battery that powers the whole device. Older Palm devices used AAA batteries for primary power. However, you could change the AAA batteries, and if you were fast enough (you usually had a minute to make the swap), you didn't lose any of your data. The reason you didn't lose your data is that the older Palms had a small rechargeable battery that powered the memory when you swapped the primary batteries. The rechargeable battery recharged itself off of a trickle charge from the AAAs.

General Notes

Your Palm device will stop turning on before the batteries are completely exhausted. This gives you a chance to recharge them (or swap them if you are using AAAs) before you lose your data. Typically, you have about a week from the time your Palm device stops turning on until you will lose your data. If you should happen to lose your data, you can always restore the data from your most recent HotSync.

> Your Palm device will eventually drain batteries (even full batteries) even if you don't turn it on. It takes power to keep the memory intact, which pulls from the batteries. A powered-off Palm can drain its batteries within a month or so for rechargeables and a bit longer for alkalines.

Replacing Rechargeable Batteries

Replacing rechargeable batteries will likely void the warranty on your Palm device. If your PDA is still under warranty, you are better off having them fix it—not least because your problem might not be a bad battery at all. If your device isn't under warranty, then you can end up paying as much to have it fixed as you paid to buy it in the first place. You would be better off buying a replacement device on eBay! However, you can search on Google for a replacement battery—just type the model of your device and "replacement battery" (e.g., m515 replacement battery). You should be able to find a new battery online for about $25. You should also buy the appropriate screwdriver to open your device, if you don't already have one, such as a Torx T5.

Before you go through the work of replacing it, you should check to see if the problem you are having is caused by the battery. If your device can power on with the AC adapter inserted, but it won't come up (or it only comes up for a very short time) if you are only using the battery (despite being recharged for several hours), then the problem is most likely the battery. It could be something that is harder to fix, such as the connection from the battery to the Palm device [Hack #54], but the battery is a strong possibility in this case. One other experiment to try before you replace the battery is to reset your device while it is on AC power. This can sometimes reset the charging circuitry which might be the only problem. See *http://kb.palmone. com/SRVS/CGI-BIN/WEBCGI.EXE?New,Kb=PalmSupportKB,ts=Palm_ External2001,case=obj(887)#incradle* for an example.

> Replacing the main rechargeable battery will cause your Palm device to lose all data and all applications other than the built-in ones. If possible, try to HotSync to make sure that your PC has the latest available copies of the data on your Palm device.

Locate and open the battery compartment on the back of your Palm device. This may require a special screwdriver such as a mini Phillips or a Torx T5. Open the battery compartment and examine the battery. You need to find out what kind of battery it is so you can buy the appropriate replacement. Figure 8-10 shows a Palm m515 being opened up, and Figure 8-11 shows the Palm with its cover off. The battery is connected to the mainboard by two short wires, one red and one black.

Next, unplug the battery from the mainboard and remove it from the case, as shown in Figure 8-12. You can now plug the new battery into the connector (see Figure 8-13), install it, and reassemble the Palm.

If your device uses AAAs, then you still might need to change the small rechargeable battery that powers the device while you are changing the AAAs. If you find that your device always loses memory when you change the primary batteries, regardless of how quickly you change over the batteries, then it is possible that the rechargeable battery has failed. These are readily available-they are typically a small button battery that you can find in electronics stores. The trick on this is to make sure that you have fresh AAAs installed in your PDA, then open up your device to expose the button battery. Unless there is a marked compartment on the back, you will probably need to remove the entire back cover. Inside, you should find a small battery. Take it with you to the store so that you can get the same kind of battery as a replacement. After installing the replacement battery, you should be able to switch AAAs (quickly) without losing your data.

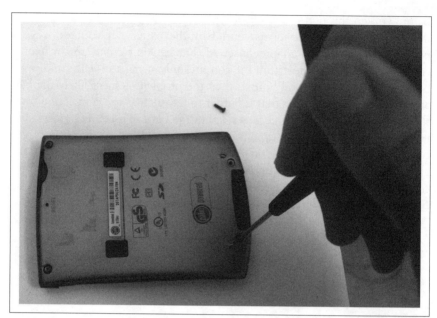

Figure 8-10. Opening a Palm m515

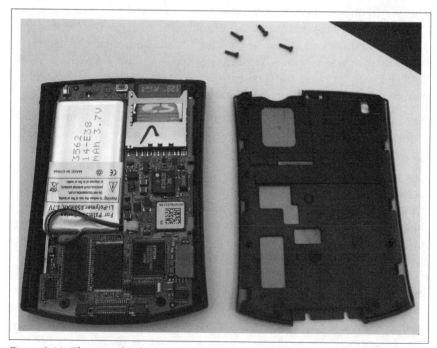

Figure 8-11. The opened Palm

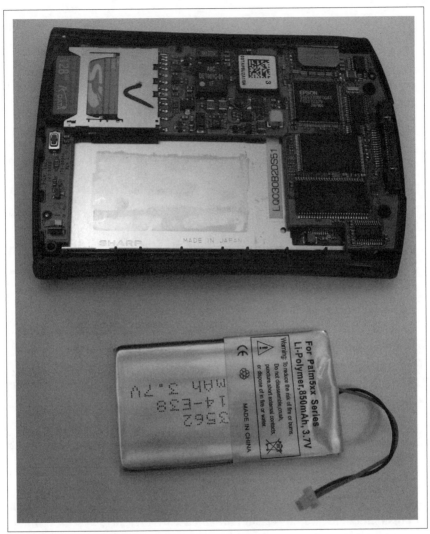

Figure 8-12. Removing the old battery

Be sure to dispose of the old battery properly. The U.S. electronics chain Best Buy will accept many types of rechargeable batteries for recycling, and several other chains and programs will do the same. For more information, see the Rechargeable Battery Recycling Corporation's web site (*http://www.rbrc.org/*).

Figure 8-13. Installing the new battery

Finding Replacement Batteries

There are some web sites which have replacement batteries available for various models of Palm devices. The batteries are very specific to which model of device you have, so you need to look around carefully.

- *http://www.cliebattery.com* lists batteries for different Clié models.
- *http://palm.pdainternalbattery.com* lists batteries for various Palm-brand devices, including Treos.
- *http://store.everythingtreo.com* also lists batteries for Treos

Another good resource for batteries are lightly used Palms **[Hack #50]**. A couple of possibilities are swap meets and *http://www.freecycle.org*. In both of these, you can look for a similar model to the one you have which has a working battery. You may have to take the devices that are offered and swap the battery (and recharge it) to see if you can salvage a working device.

Index

We'd like to hear your suggestions for improving our indexes. Send email to *index@oreilly.com*.

B

Baen Free Library, 84
BalanceLog, 37
batteries, 202–206
  AAA, 202
  disposing, 205
  finding replacements, 206
  Rechargeable Battery Recycling
    Corporation, 205
  replacing rechargeable, 202
BeiksFind, 19
Bejeweled, 70
binary tracking, 31
Blogger, 145, 146, 147
Bloglines, 143
blogs, 144–147
  HBlogger, 145
  mo:Blog, 145
  Plogit, 146
  remote access software, 145
  SplashBlog, 146
  Vagablog, 147
Bluetooth, 125–131
  cell phone, 125
  connections, 71
  DUN, 110
    enabling on Treo 650, 111
    shadowmite patch, 111
  LAN Access Point, 125
  troubleshooting, 131
  Windows XP computer as an access
    point, 126–131
Blunty, 145
Breakout, 78
Brighthand, 194
ButtonLauncher, 168

C

cables, finding online, 124
calculators, 47–48
  APCalc, 47
  EasyCalc, 47
  powerOne Scientific, 47
  using for gaming, 80
  using spreadsheets as, 44
Caleida, 145
cameras (see digital cameras)
CardScan, 197
Cartoforge, 61, 65

CaSTaway, 75
CDMA devices, 133
cell phones, 125
  acting as modem connection to the
    Internet, 124
Centipede, 78
Chatter Email, 137
Chess, 68
ChessGenius, 72
Cingular Wireless, 112, 133, 139
Circuit Writer Pen, 200
Code Jedi web site, 27
collectible inventory systems, 25–28
  database approach, 27
  HandyShopper, 27
  MemoPad, 25
  ShadowPlan, 26
Comfort Stylus, 193
communications, 122–159
computer swap meets, 191
connections
  reparing worn, 198–200
CoursePro course management
    application, 25
cradle, connection to the Internet, 123
Creative Commons, 91
Cross MicroPen stylus, 193
cross-compiler, 56
CSLIP, 123
CSpotRun, 83

D

Daggerware web site, 175
Data Import application, Disconnect
    and, 11
data, importing into desktop, 17
Date Book application, 1–4, 38
  alarms, 4
  floating events, 3
  new item, creating, 6
  no time events, 3
  Purge events, 4
  repeating events, 2
  to do items, 1
  Today view, 1
DateBk5, 3
DDH Software web site, 28
DeadJournal, 145
Decuma, 86, 88

Colophon

Our look is the result of reader comments, our own experimentation, and feedback from distribution channels. Distinctive covers complement our distinctive approach to technical topics, breathing personality and life into potentially dry subjects.

The tools on the cover of *Palm and Treo Hacks* are a Palm and a Treo. The PalmPilot was invented in 1996 by Jeff Hawkins, Donna Dubinsky, and Ed Colligan, founders of Palm Computing. Hired to develop handwriting recognition software for a handheld device, members of the development team began to see greater possibilities. Once the software was finished, they turned their attention to better hardware design. Hawkins tested the size of a potential portable device by carrying a block of wood in his pocket. Before long, the PalmPilot was born. Hawkins went on to oversee the licensing of the Palm OS.

The PalmPilot is now merging with smartphone technology such as that offered by the Treo, which adds cell phone, email, and instant messaging functionality to the handheld device.

Adam Witwer was the production editor and Nancy Reinhardt was the copyeditor for *Palm and Treo Hacks*. Jeffrey Liggett proofread the text. Abby Fox and Claire Cloutier provided quality control. Julie Hawks wrote the index.

Marcia Friedman designed the cover of this book, based on a series design by Edie Freedman. Karen Montgomery produced the cover layout with Adobe InDesign CS using Adobe's Helvetica Neue and ITC Garamond fonts.

David Futato designed the interior layout. This book was converted by Keith Fahlgren to FrameMaker 5.5.6 with a format conversion tool created by Erik Ray, Jason McIntosh, Neil Walls, and Mike Sierra that uses Perl and XML technologies. The text font is Linotype Birka; the heading font is Adobe Helvetica Neue Condensed; and the code font is LucasFont's TheSans Mono Condensed. The illustrations that appear in the book were produced by Robert Romano, Jessamyn Read, and Lesley Borash using Macromedia FreeHand MX and Adobe Photoshop CS. This colophon was written by Adam Witwer.

Better than e-books

Buy *Palm & Treo Hacks* and access the
digital edition FREE on Safari for 45 days.

Go to www.oreilly.com/go/safarienabled
and type in coupon code AZLB-HJXM-H2Z8-DUMF-LPP7

Search
thousands of
top tech books

Download
whole chapters

Cut and Paste
code examples

Find
answers fast

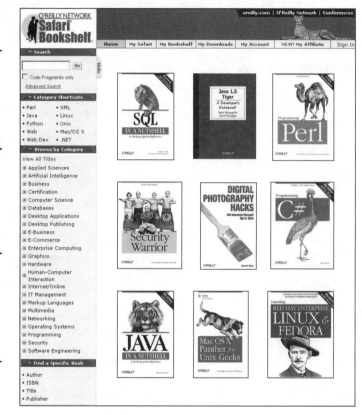

Search Safari! The premier electronic reference
library for programmers and IT professionals.

Related Titles from O'Reilly

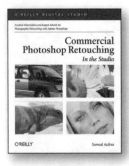

Digital Media

Adobe Creative Suite
CS2 Workflow

Adobe InDesign CS2
One-on-One

Adobe Encore DVD:
In the Studio

Adobe Photoshop CS2
One-on-One

Assembling Panoramic
Photos: A Designer's
Notebook

Creating Photomontages
with Photoshop:
A Designer's Notebook

Commercial Photoshop
Retouching: In the Studio

The DAM Book: Digital
Asset Management for
Photographers

Digital Photography:
Expert Techniques

Digital Photography Hacks

Digital Photography Pocket
Guide, *3rd Edition*

Digital Video Pocket Guide

Digital Video Hacks

DV Filmmaking: From Start
to Finish

DVD Studio Pro 3:
In the Studio

GarageBand 2: The Missing
Manual, *2nd Edition*

Home Theater Hacks

Illustrations with Photoshop:
A Designer's Notebook

iMovie HD & iDVD 5:
The Missing Manual

iPhoto 5: The Missing
Manual, *4th Edition*

iPod & iTunes Hacks

iPod & iTunes: The Missing
Manual, *3rd Edition*

iPod Fan Book

iPod Playlists

iPod Shuffle Fan Book

Photo Retouching with
Photoshop: A Designer's
Notebook

Photoshop Elements 3 for
Windows One-on-One

Photoshop Elements 3:
The Missing Manual

Photoshop Photo Effects
Cookbook

Photoshop Raw

Photoshop Retouching
Cookbook for Digital
Photographers

Windows Media Hacks

Keep in touch with O'Reilly

Download examples from our books

To find example files from a book, go to: *www.oreilly.com/catalog* select the book, and follow the "Examples" link.

Register your O'Reilly books

Register your book at *register.oreilly.com* Why register your books? Once you've registered your O'Reilly books you can:

- Win O'Reilly books, T-shirts or discount coupons in our monthly drawing.

- Get special offers available only to registered O'Reilly customers.

- Get catalogs announcing new books (US and UK only).

- Get email notification of new editions of the O'Reilly books you own.

Join our email lists

Sign up to get topic-specific email announcements of new books and conferences, special offers, and O'Reilly Network technology newsletters at:

elists.oreilly.com

It's easy to customize your free elists subscription so you'll get exactly the O'Reilly news you want.

Get the latest news, tips, and tools

www.oreilly.com

- "Top 100 Sites on the Web"—PC Magazine
- CIO Magazine's Web Business 50 Awards

Our web site contains a library of comprehensive product information (including book excerpts and tables of contents), downloadable software, background articles, interviews with technology leaders, links to relevant sites, book cover art, and more.

Work for O'Reilly

Check out our web site for current employment opportunities:

jobs.oreilly.com

Contact us

O'Reilly Media, Inc.
1005 Gravenstein Hwy North
Sebastopol, CA 95472 USA
Tel: 707-827-7000 or 800-998-9938
  (6am to 5pm PST)
Fax: 707-829-0104

Contact us by email

For answers to problems regarding your order or our products:
order@oreilly.com

To request a copy of our latest catalog:
catalog@oreilly.com

For book content technical questions or corrections: **booktech@oreilly.com**

For educational, library, government, and corporate sales: **corporate@oreilly.com**

To submit new book proposals to our editors and product managers:
proposals@oreilly.com

For information about our international distributors or translation queries:
international@oreilly.com

For information about academic use of O'Reilly books:
adoption@oreilly.com
or visit:
academic.oreilly.com

For a list of our distributors outside of North America check out:
international.oreilly.com/distributors.html

Order a book online

www.oreilly.com/order_new